WORKBOOK VOLUME A

FOCUS ON GRAMMAR

An **ADVANCED** Course for Reference and Practice

SECOND EDITION

Rachel Spack Koch with **Keith S. Folse**

Longman

FOCUS ON GRAMMAR: AN ADVANCED COURSE FOR REFERENCE AND PRACTICE
WORKBOOK VOLUME A

Copyright © 2000, 1994 by Addison Wesley Longman, Inc.
A Pearson Education Company.
All rights reserved.
No part of this publication may be reproduced,
stored in a retrieval system, or transmitted
in any form or by any means, electronic, mechanical,
photocopying, recording, or otherwise,
without the prior permission of the publisher.

Pearson Education, 10 Bank Street, White Plains, NY 10606

Editorial director: Allen Ascher
Executive editor: Louisa Hellegers
Director of design and production: Rhea Banker
Development editor: Bill Preston
Production manager: Alana Zdinak
Managing editor: Linda Moser
Production editor: Robert Ruvo
Senior manufacturing manager: Patrice Fraccio
Manufacturing manager: David Dickey
Cover design: Rhea Banker
Text design adaptation: Rainbow Graphics
Text composition: Rainbow Graphics

0–201–38315–2

1 2 3 4 5 6 7 8 9 10—BAH—04 03 02 01 00

Contents

PART I   TENSE AND TIME
UNIT 1   Present and Future Time   1
UNIT 2   Past Time   9
UNIT 3   Past, Present, and Future   18

PART II   MODALS
UNIT 4   Modals: Necessity   31
UNIT 5   Modals: Certainty   41

PART III   NOUNS
UNIT 6   Count and Non-Count Nouns   52
UNIT 7   Definite and Indefinite Articles   60
UNIT 8   Modification of Nouns   71
UNIT 9   Quantifiers   78

PART IV   ADJECTIVE CLAUSES AND PHRASES
UNIT 10   Adjective Clauses: Review and Expansion   86
UNIT 11   Adjective Clauses with Quantifiers; Adjectival Modifying Phrases   98

PART V   PASSIVE VOICE
UNIT 12   The Passive: Review and Expansion   106
UNIT 13   Reporting Ideas and Facts with Passives   117

ANSWER KEY   AK1

TESTS
UNITS   1–3   T1
UNITS   4–5   T5
UNITS   6–9   T9
UNITS   10–11   T12
UNITS   12–13   T16

ANSWER KEY FOR TESTS   T20

ABOUT THE AUTHORS

Rachel Spack Koch has been developing ESL materials and has taught ESL for many years, principally at the University of Miami, and also at Harvard University, Bellevue Community College, and Miami-Dade Community College. In addition to *Focus on Grammar: An Advanced Course for Reference and Practice Workbook,* she has contributed to other widely used ESL workbooks. She has written structure and writing questions for the TOEFL and for test preparation materials. An early participant and developer of interactive student activities on the Internet, she also designs and writes content for ESL software.

Keith S. Folse has taught English for more than twenty years in many places, including the United States, Saudi Arabia, Kuwait, Malaysia, and Japan. He has a Ph.D. in Second Language Acquisition and Instructional Technology. He has written fifteen other ESL books on grammar, composition, reading, speaking, and TOEFL. He regularly does workshops and presentations for teachers all over the world.

PART | TENSE AND TIME

UNIT 1

PRESENT AND FUTURE TIME

1 USING VERB TENSES

A new play is opening tonight. The curtain rises as we see Paul, a new father, talking and singing to his three-week-old daughter. It's midnight. Fill in the blanks with the correct form of the verbs in parentheses.

Oh, little daughter! You are the best thing that ____has come____
1. (is coming / has come)
into our lives. We _____ such a wonderful life together.
2. (are going to have / have had)
Soon you _____, then you _____
3. ('ll be walking / 're walking)   4. ('ll go / 've gone)
to school, and you _____ friends. The next thing you know,
5. (will have / have)
I _____ down the aisle with you at your wedding.
6. (will be walking / am going to walk)
Oh, little one! Time flies! Too soon you _____
7. (will have grown / will have been growing)
up and _____ a life of your own, with children
8. (will have had / will be having)
of your own. I _____ a grandfather. But I
9. (am / will be)
_____ about your life too far into the future. We
10. (am thinking / think)
_____ a lot of years between now and then.
11. (have / are having)

He hums and sings:

Hush, little baby, don't say a word,

Papa _____ you a mockingbird.
12. ('s going to buy / buys)
And if that mockingbird _____,
13. (doesn't sing / isn't singing)
Papa _____ you a diamond ring.
14. ('s going to buy / 's buying)
Shh! Shh! Why _____? Everything's going
15. (do you cry / are you crying)
to be just fine.

2 DISTINGUISHING ACTIONS IN THE PRESENT AND FUTURE TIME

*The following is a letter from Goodman and Greene, a financial planning firm. In each set of two sentences, write **1** in front of the action that happened first, and **2** in front of the action that happened second.*

Dear Professional:

As you read this, retirement seems very far away.

1. You have a good income, and you're getting a nice raise in January.
   - _1_ You have a good income.
   - _2_ You get a nice raise in January.

2. If you save a little more this year, you'll be able to buy a new home soon.
   - ___ You save a little more.
   - ___ You are able to buy a new home.

3. You can take a long vacation as soon as you have the time.
   - ___ You can take a long vacation.
   - ___ You have the time.

4. By the time your children are ready for college, you will have saved enough money for their tuition.
   - ___ Your children are ready for college.
   - ___ You have the money you need for their tuition.

5. When you retire, you will have been working steadily for 35 years.
   - ___ You retire.
   - ___ You work steadily.

6. You will have earned the comfortable life that you are dreaming about.
   - ___ You earn the comfortable life.
   - ___ You dream about the comfortable life.

7. However, you need to plan carefully long before you retire.
   - ___ You retire.
   - ___ You plan carefully.

   Call our office today for an appointment with one of our experienced financial planners. He or she will discuss your unique situation with you and suggest which mix of stocks, bonds, and other financial instruments are best for you.

8. After you have met with him or her, you will feel confident about your financial future.
   - ___ You meet with him or her.
   - ___ You feel confident.

Sincerely yours,

Boris M. Goodman

Boris M. Goodman, President

3 DISTINGUISHING ACTIONS IN THE PRESENT AND FUTURE TIME

*Lucia has written an e-mail to her close friend Thelma, asking for advice about a personal ad she is placing. Over each underlined phrase, indicate whether the time refers to the **Present (P)** or **Future (F)**. Add a check mark (✓) if the time includes reference to the past.*

Hi, Thelma:

    I'm putting (F) an ad in the Personals and I've written (P✓) one (it's attached). I don't think it has enough pizzazz, so I'm sending it to you now in the hopes that you can improve it. I was thinking of putting it on the Net because that way I'd get some quick responses, but I think I'll get more quality people to respond if I put it in a literary or more sophisticated publication. Besides, that will give me time to lose some weight. By the time the ad appears in the Personals, I will have lost about 10 pounds, and I'll be a size 8 again.

    A new issue is coming out next Tuesday, but I've missed the deadline. The ad will appear in the issue after this one, which comes out at the beginning of December.

    Hurry! I'll be waiting for your reply. Thanks in advance for your help!

Lucia

Attachment:

    I'm looking for the man of my dreams: a tall, strong, and caring man who wants to share his life with someone special. I may be that someone. I am slim and pretty, with fluffy blond hair. I swim, ski, sail, and play tennis. I've belonged to the Village Poetry Group for seven years, and I play Scrabble. I've lived a lot and loved a little, and now I want to love a lot. Are you the one I'm looking for?

4 USING VERB TENSES

Here is a letter from a tour operator, just prior to a group's departure for Antarctica. In each blank space, write the correct form of the verb in parentheses.

Destination: Antarctica

Dear Traveler:

Enclosed are your tickets, your itinerary, your luggage tags, and the passenger list for your trip to Argentina and Antarctica on the 30th of this month. We know that this is going to be the trip of your life!

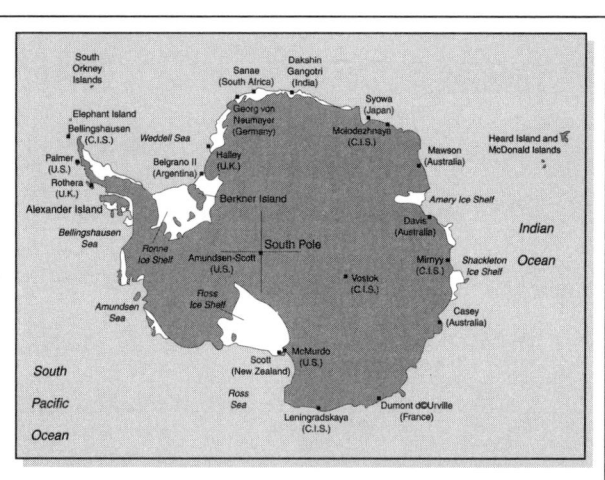

We will meet in the *GlobeAir* lounge in Miami when everybody ___arrives___ from other flights. After we _____ each other at a small "Welcome Aboard"
                                             1. (arrive)   2. (greet)
party, we'll depart for Buenos Aires. As soon as you _____ the ship, you
                                                                     3. (board)
_____ the adventure in the air!
   4. (feel)

After a one-day stopover in Buenos Aires, we'll continue on to Antarctica. As you _____ into the world's most unspoiled continent, you'll see penguins, glaciers,
  5. (venture)
and spectacular scenery. You'll marvel at the clear, cold air and the stunning high mountains. Our experienced naturalists will describe the area before you actually _____ the bays by small landing craft.
  6. (explore)

After we _____ at sea for two weeks, you _____ to return to
                 7. (be)   8. (want / not)
your normal routine. You _____ unique sights and adventures for the past
                         9. (experience)
two weeks. By the time you _____ to Buenos Aires on the 15th, you
                          10. (return)
_____ the ultimate in adventure cruising.
  11. (experience)

I look forward to meeting you all and to our exciting trip together!

Truly yours,

Margaret de Bono

Margaret de Bono, Cruise Director

5 USING TENSES IN SENTENCES WITH FUTURE TIME CLAUSES

In Beautiville Central High School, elections were held for the following distinctions and won by the following people. These results appeared in the BCHS yearbook. Following this list, there is an article projecting the future for these graduates. Fill in the blanks with the correct tenses of the verbs in parentheses.

Title	Winner
Most Likely to Succeed	Al Albert
Funniest	Ed Edelman
Best Looking	Deirdre Denson
Most Athletic	Fred Fenson
Best Dressed	Gail George
Most Popular	Harry Hernández
Best Dancer	Izzy Igua
Best Natured	Jenny James
Cleverest	Katherine Klumper
Class Sweethearts	Rose Rincón and Bob Bradley

HERE'S WHAT WE CAN EXPECT FROM OUR GRADUATING SENIORS IN THE NEXT DECADE.

There is no doubt that Al Albert will be a fine lawyer. Whenever the famous criminals ____need____ the best legal defense, Al will be there in court. Our
1. (need)

class comedian, Ed Edelman, will no doubt be the most popular of the stand-up comics. When the awards for the best television comedy star _____
2. (be)

given in ten years, it is certain that Ed will win one. And our own beautiful Deirdre Denson is going to win a very coveted award: the Miss America Contest. We are sure that within the next five years, our Deirdre _____ Miss
3. (be)

America. The Most Valuable Player of the American League? Fred Fenson

_____ that award for being the best player of the year before the
4. (receive)

decade _____ over.
5. (be)

(continued on next page)

Unit 1

It should come as no surprise that the best-dressed person in our graduating class, Gail George, has accepted a job at *Gorgeous Magazine*; we fully expect that before five years _____ by, she will be well known in the fashion field.
6. (go)
Whatever Harry Hernández does and wherever he goes, he will have friends. As the most popular person in our class, Harry is sure to succeed in whatever career he undertakes after we _____. Another popular guy who is also our
7. (graduate)
best dancer, Izzy Igua is destined to become very famous in musical theater. He _____ in a big role in the dancing troupe of *Cats*; he has already signed
8. (star)
a contract to begin the week after graduation.

There is no doubt that our dear Jenny James _____ welcomed and
9. (be)
loved wherever she goes during the next hundred years; she is so good-natured that everyone adores her. And our clever Katherine Klumper? She is going to be a financial wizard. About to enter Cornell University as a sophomore when the fall semester _____, she plans to get both her B.A. and M.B.A. within
10. (start)
four years. There are two people we feel especially fond of: Rose Rincón and Bob Bradley, our class sweethearts. They _____ together for five
11. (go)
years; we know that they _____ a lifetime of happiness after they
12. (have)
_____ married next month.
13. (get)
So, what _____ during the next ten years? What careers will we be
14. (we / all / do)
engaged in? How will we fare as spouses and parents? Stay in touch, and come to our tenth class reunion. By that time, we _____, _____, or
15. (work)   16. (study)
_____ house for ten years, and we certainly _____ a lot to
17. (keep)   18. (have)
talk about on that reunion night in ten years!

6 EDITING

Marco has written to Ricardo, his friend back home. Find and correct the seventeen errors in verb forms.

> Dear Ricardo:
>
>   I ~~am~~ *have been* here in the United States for two months now. Classes in my intensive English program in Chicago began about six weeks ago. The instructors has given homework every day, and I have been studying a lot. In fact, I study right now because I have a big test tomorrow. So far, I do well in class, and I hope to continue.
>
>   Even more than in class, I learn a great deal of English by talking with people in the city. In my apartment building, most people are speaking English, and when I need something, I have to speak to the manager in English. For example, my bathroom faucet wasn't working, and I had to explain the problem. I did! The plumber is coming on Tuesday!
>
>   On the negative side, the food is not being as good as at home, and the weather is quite bad this month. It's raining almost every day. In addition, sometimes I feel lonely. I didn't meet many friendly people so far, and I hadn't been having much fun. So, please write me soon! It always is making me feel good to hear from you.
>
>   I'm very happy to be home again next year. When I will leave here, I will had been studying English for a year and, hopefully, will have learn a lot. By this time next year I have finished my studies forever, and I'll work with my dad in his office. With luck I learn English well, and that will be helpful in Dad's business.
>
>   Your friend,
>   Marco

7 PERSONALIZATION

Write about your life, using some of the phrases in the box.

> So far, my life . . .
> Since I graduated from high school, . . .
> For the past two years, . . .
> Right now . . .
> Very soon, . . .
> In fact, next week . . .
> At the end of next year, . . .
> By the end of next year, . . .
> In ten years, . . .
> By the time I am old, . . .

UNIT 2

PAST TIME

1 USING VERB TENSES

In the following article from a magazine on demographics, select the correct verb form in each set of parentheses.

When people think of the stereotypical American, what do they imagine? They usually picture a pleasant, big, blond football player, whose ancestors _____arrived_____ in the New World
1. (arrived / were arriving)
from northern Europe in the eighteenth or early nineteenth century. Although a great number of Americans indeed _____
2. (came / were coming)
from northern Europe, the current population is actually composed of groups from all over the world. Large numbers of southern and eastern Europeans _____ to arrive in the
3. (have begun / began)
United States before the end of the nineteenth century; thus, there are now, for example, many well-established Italian, Greek, Portuguese, Polish, and Armenian communities. Asians _____ to immigrate even before then. In
4. (have begun / had begun)
recent decades, other Asians and people from Central and South America and the Caribbean _____ in
5. (have been arriving / had been arriving)
large numbers. Like the earlier arrivals, these new immigrants _____ among their countrymen in
6. (would settle / had settled)
established communities.

(continued on next page)

With the waves of immigrants _____ new languages,
7. (came / were coming)
customs, and foods. Especially in recent years, Italian, Mexican, Chinese, Thai, and Japanese restaurants _____ up all over the country; pizza,
8. (have sprung / had sprung)
fajitas, dim sum, and sushi, which _____ considered
9. (used to be / would be)
foreign dishes, are now as American as apple pie. Many Spanish words—for example, *amigo, siesta, adios,* and *macho*—have become an integral part of most Americans' vocabulary, just as the English language itself _____ with
10. (had come / would come)
the original settlers from England and _____ throughout
11. (spread / used to spread)
the land.

The real America is a mix of many cultures. In the past, people thought that eventually various groups _____ into one culture, but in
12. (used to assimilate / would assimilate)
fact the opposite _____: There are many and varied cultural
13. (has occurred / had occurred)
communities coexisting in mainstream America today.

2 ORDERING ACTIONS IN PAST TIME

*Harry Williams is a retired professor who lives alone. This morning he discovered that an intruder had entered his house during the night. He told this story to the police. Indicate the order of the actions in Harry's story by writing **1** or **2** on the line before each sentence. In making your selection, consider the <u>beginning</u> of each action. If the actions happened at the same time, write **S** on both lines.*

1. When I got up this morning, I found that a large glass door had been broken during the night.

   __2__ Harry got up.

   __1__ A door had been broken.

2. It appeared that a thief had entered the house while I was sleeping.

   ____ A thief had entered the house.

   ____ He was sleeping.

3. I looked around the house and found that the drawers of my desk were open.

   ____ He found the drawers open.

   ____ Harry looked around the house.

4. Worriedly, I ran to my desk and discovered that my passport was missing.
   ___ He ran to his desk.
   ___ He discovered that his passport was missing.
5. After I searched further, I realized that my keys were gone, too.
   ___ He realized that his keys were gone.
   ___ He searched further.
6. While I was dialing the police, someone rang the bell.
   ___ He was dialing the police.
   ___ Someone rang the bell.
7. When I opened the door, I saw my neighbor. He smiled and handed me my keys.
   ___ Harry opened the door.
   ___ His neighbor handed him his keys.
8. "I found these on the sidewalk," my neighbor said. "Thank you so much," I said. "And by the way, have you seen my passport?" "Your passport? No. You told me you had sent it in for renewal."
   ___ Harry told the neighbor something.
   ___ Harry sent in his passport for renewal.
9. "Oh, right! I did! I completely forgot," I said. "I thought that someone had stolen it, along with my keys."
   ___ Harry thought something.
   ___ Someone stole his passport and keys, he believed.
10. "Oh, Harry! You've done it again! You are a totally absent-minded professor!" he said. I smiled. "I guess I am. Won't you come in?" I asked my neighbor.
    ___ Harry smiled.
    ___ He invited his neighbor into the house.

3 USING VERB TENSES

This is part of a memoir written by a young woman. Choose the correct form of the verb in parentheses for each of the blank spaces.

My parents and I came to live in the United States when I was five years old. Although my family is now very comfortable, at first we had a hard time adjusting to life here. We _____had thought_____ that everybody in America was very rich. Imagine our
1. (had thought / were thinking)
surprise when we _____ that it was hard for many people, my
2. (learned / were learning)
father included, to make a living.

My father _____ as a dentist in Europe before we
3. (had been working / has been working)
_____ here thirty-three years ago. Here he couldn't work as a
4. (have come / came)

(continued on next page)

dentist right away because he _____ the state examinations
5. (hadn't been passing / hadn't passed)
yet. While he _____ for the dentist examinations, he
6. (had studied / was studying)
_____ in a dental laboratory in order to support his family.
7. (worked / had worked)

Within a year, he _____ the examinations and
8. (was passing / had passed)
_____ himself in practice with a local dentist. He had a long
9. (established / used to establish)
and successful career as a dentist. By the time he _____ last
10. (retired / was retiring)
year, he _____ dentistry for thirty years. During his career, he
11. (was practicing / had been practicing)
earned the respect of his peers and the devotion of his patients, as well as the love of the
poor immigrants to whom he _____ his services free of charge.
12. (used to contribute / was contributing)

My mother, too, _____ happy here. She
13. (has been / had been)
_____ a degree in finance five years ago, and she now owns and
14. (got / has gotten)
operates her own profitable copy center. She _____ courses
15. (has been taking / had been taking)
for a long time before she actually _____ her degree. She
16. (got / had gotten)
_____ only one or two courses each semester because she was
17. (would take / has taken)
busy looking after my father, my brother, and me. Now she is an independent woman who
runs her own business.

I myself _____ a wonderful life. Three years ago I
18. (have been having / had had)
_____ my law degree, and since then I
19. (got / had gotten)
_____ in a small law firm where I am very happy. I know the
20. (have been working / was working)
partners of the firm quite well, as I _____ here in the summers
21. (used to work / was working)
when I was in law school. While I _____ here one summer, I
22. (worked / was working)
_____ a terrific man, whom I married the following year. He
23. (met / was meeting)
doesn't work here anymore; he _____ a judge and is well
24. (was becoming / became)
respected in the community.

My family and I faced some difficulties when we first _____
25. (arrived / were arriving)
in this country because we _____ things to be as difficult as
26. (hadn't expected / haven't expected)
they in fact were. We didn't know then what we know now: that we
_____ beyond our wildest dreams.
27. (used to succeed / would succeed)

4 USING VERB TENSES

Lila has written an e-mail to her sister Annie complaining about her husband, Craig. In each blank space, write the correct verb form chosen from the box below.

buy	is
call	making
~~cut~~	promises
didn't	take
fix	was going to
has	will
hasn't	

Promises! Promises!

I'll never believe another thing that Craig tells me. Last week he told me that he would ____cut____ the grass, but he hasn't done it yet. Then he said that he was going to
1.
_____ the leaky faucet in the kitchen, but it _____ still dripping.
2.   3.
He promised that he would _____ my mother to wish her a happy birthday,
4.
but he _____ done that, either.
5.
He thinks I'll feel better if he _____ to buy me an expensive gift. He told me
6.
that he was going to _____ me a big surprise on Valentine's Day, but he
7.
_____ even send a card. Our anniversary is next month, and he said that
8.
he was _____ reservations at a fancy hotel to spend the weekend, but
9.
I'll bet that he _____ forgotten all about it. He even promised that he
10.
_____ give me a car for my birthday, but he didn't say which birthday. There
11.
is one thing I know that he will do: nap. He told me that he would _____ a
12.
nap this afternoon, and I'm sure that he _____ take one!
13.

5 USING VERB TENSES

The following newspaper article tells about a special anniversary. In each blank space, write the correct form of the verb in parentheses.

WEDDING ANNOUNCEMENTS

A second wedding anniversary celebration was held in the Downtown Center Hotel last night for Helena K. Messenger and Julius Lister. A group of 250 people, including the couple's eight children, were in attendance. The story of how these two amazing people met so late in their lives is most interesting.

Helena K. Messenger is anything but a stereotypical senior citizen. Her hair is naturally black and curly, and she drives very, very fast, zooming up her long driveway like a teenager. She ____runs____ a mile every day, takes
1. (run)
aerobic exercise classes, and appears to have none of the usual fears that come with age: Neither extra-spicy food nor loneliness concern her at all.

After her husband _____
2. (die)
in 1983, she _____ living in
3. (continue)
their big, creaky house in New Jersey, surrounded by quiet, empty rooms. In 1990, while she _____ a
4. (attend)
singles discussion group, someone _____ her to Julius Lister.
5. (introduce)
Mr. Lister works full time as an engineer in one of the army's research centers. He has several hobbies, including windsurfing, canoeing, and hiking. Mr. Lister _____ his wife in 1989, and just
6. (lose)
before he _____ Ms. Messenger
7. (meet)
he _____ dating again, without
8. (begin)
much success. One of his daughters recalled, "He _____ out with
9. (go)
women from time to time, but he said it was very depressing."

After the meeting, Ms. Messenger _____ Mr. Lister a postcard
10. (send)
saying that she _____ to see
11. (like)
him again. As soon as he _____
12. (receive)
the postcard, he _____ and
13. (call)
_____ her to dinner. The rest is
14. (invite)

history. Since then, they _____ life more than they _____ until
              15. (spend)   17. (be)
almost all of their time together. They   that time, but neither one expected to

_____ to many parts of the   be enjoying it so completely. Much to
16. (travel)
world during the past two years. When   everyone's delight, they are indeed living

they married, they expected to be enjoying happily ever after.*

*Based on an article from *The New York Times,* July 26, 1998, by Lois Smith Brady. Names have been changed.

6 EDITING

In the following article from a magazine about biographies, there are nineteen errors in verb forms referring to the past time. Find and correct these errors.

Albert Einstein, one of the world's most renowned scientists, was born in Germany in 1879. It is said that he ~~wasn't talking~~ *didn't talk* until he was four years old, and that his parents and others believed that he was of average intelligence, or less. When he was in elementary school, his teachers hadn't thought he was a promising student. By the time he was eight years old, they have already decided that he could not learn as fast as his classmates could. Furthermore, he didn't had much interest in his classes, and he will not give time to studying the required Latin and Greek.

The only subject that interested him was mathematics. However, even this interest caused trouble with his teachers; Einstein has been solving mathematical problems in his own way which was different from the way of the prescribed curriculum. His teachers don't believe that his future will be very bright.

(continued on next page)

When Einstein was sixteen, he left school. His parents were moving to Italy earlier, so he decided to follow them there. After he is in Italy for only a few months, he decided to enter another school, the Zurich Polytechnic, in Switzerland. There he encountered other problems: the teachers forced him to study the same subjects that the other students study at the time. Of course, he already mastered the basic subjects that were taught in the school, and so he quickly had become bored and disillusioned. He has been studying physics and other natural sciences by himself before that time, and he had hoped to continue in his own way. After many frustrations, he finally has graduated from the Polytechnic just after he turned twenty-one years old. At that time, he began publishing his important scientific theories. At first, his theories weren't accepted, but after a while, other scientists were realizing how brilliant they were, and Einstein received the recognition he deserved.

Einstein settled in the United States before World War II. He taught at Princeton University in New Jersey, and continued to make important contributions to science. In the town of Princeton, he used to walking around town like any ordinary citizen, and was usually not recognized as the great man that he was.

Einstein's theories changed the ways that scientists were thinking about time, space, and matter. His ideas, such as the theory of relativity, continue to be valid today. There has been no other scientist of such importance in the twentieth century, and indeed, he is among the few great scientists of all time.

7 PERSONALIZATION

Write a brief history of the life of one of your parents, using some of the phrases in the box.

> When my father (my mother) was born, his (her) family . . .
> While he (she) was in school, . . .
> Before finishing school, . . .
> After finishing school, . . .
> His (her) first job . . .
> He (she) met my mother (my father) . . .
> Before I was born, . . .
> When I was born, . . .
> After I started school, . . .
> As a parent, . . .
> In 1998, . . .
> Since last year, . . .
> These days, . . .

UNIT 3
PAST, PRESENT, AND FUTURE

1 USING VERB TENSES

Read this article from "Just Around the Corner," a publication about things to come. Fill in the blanks with the correct form of the verbs in parentheses.

THE PERFECT PET?

Millions of people _____own_____ pets. Perhaps you
                      1. (own / are owning)
would like to own a pet, too, but, as a modern working person, you

probably _____ the time to care for one properly.
         2. (aren't having / don't have)

In earlier times, someone _____ home and was
                          3. (used to stay / has stayed)
able to take proper care of the pets; these days, however, veterinarians

_____ more and more well-meaning people who
4. (are seeing / have seen)
don't have time to attend to their pets' needs.

But, there is a way for you to enjoy a dog or a cat without the mess, the

breakage, and the ongoing care. Sony Computer Science Laboratories in

Japan _____ a little robot dog that is
      5. (develop / has developed)

approximately six inches tall and _____ three
                                  6. (weighs / is weighing)

and a half pounds, a little smaller than a Yorkshire terrier. His name is Aibo, which

_____ "companion" in Japanese, and for $2,500, he could be yours.
7. (means / is meaning)

When Aibo _____, he kneels on a recharging base. He perks
8. (is resting / has been resting)

up and wags his tail if you _____ him on a flat surface. Aibo
9. (place / will place)

_____ the color pink, and _____ after
10. (recognizes / is recognizing)   11. (will chase / is chasing)

a pink plastic ball that comes with the purchase.

Sony's technicians _____ Aibo to walk around by himself
12. (have programmed / have been programming)

and to express a few "emotions": He wags his tail or flashes his eyes in response to spoken

commands and pats on the head. Aibo also _____ back and
13. (moves / is moving)

forth in response to commands from a remote control. He will even bark if you

_____ sound files into his body. But Aibo can't do everything:
14. (download / will download)

He _____ a newspaper and he _____
15. (doesn't fetch / isn't fetching)   16. (doesn't jump / isn't jumping)

joyfully on his master with love like a real dog.

If you prefer cats, Omron and Matsushita, two large Japanese electronics

firms, _____ robot cats. Omron's cat
17. (will have already developed / have already developed)

_____ use of physical contact rather than "vision" to
18. (has made / makes)

interact with people. The cat _____ five sensors and three
19. (is using / uses)

micro-switches on its head and body to recognize a touch or a pat. This physical contact

is the signal that _____ the cat so that it purrs and responds
20. (activates / is activating)

in a friendly way.

In fact, Sony's dog and Omron's cat _____ all the right
21. (are having / have)

qualifications for being the perfect pet: They _____ any mess,
22. (don't involve / aren't involving)

they _____ anything, and they _____
23. (don't break / haven't broken)   24. (don't require / aren't requiring)

tender loving care. If you _____ pangs of loneliness these days,
25. (experience / are experiencing)

you—the modern person—can be the owner of a truly modern pet: a robo-pet.

*Adapted from Bob Johnstone, "Japan's Friendly Robots" (www.techreview.com:80/articles/may99/johnstone.htm); and Lisa Guernsey, "A Smart Dog with Megabytes," *The New York Times*, May 13, 1999.

Unit 3

2 USING VERB TENSES

Read this article on robots in Japan. Write the correct tense of the verb in parentheses.

ROBOTS IN JAPAN

When most people in the U.S. or Canada think of robots, they __imagine__ (1. imagine) large, bulky, rather unattractive creatures. In fact, many people's concept of robots is not very positive. In recent years, many movies—such as *The Terminator* and *Blade Runner*— _____ (2. portray) robots as slaves that eventually rise up to revolt against their human masters by gaining enough intelligence and power to win control of their human contacts.

Although robots may be viewed negatively in Western culture, in Japan the situation is quite different. In Japanese culture, people view robots as beneficial; stories about robots are popular. There _____ (3. be) increasing interest in robots for the past several years.

The current robot craze _____ (4. start) in 1996 when Honda Motor Corporation presented the world with P-2, a robot different from any other that _____ (5. appear) until then. P-2 looked like an astronaut. It had two legs and could walk like a human being. Unlike previous robots, P-2 had a unique battery pack which _____ (6. allow) it to walk autonomously without a power or control cord. At its debut, P-2 climbed stairs and _____ (7. give) flowers to young girls, feats that previous computers _____ (8. never accomplish).

P-2 was based on a comic book robot named Mighty Atom that appeared in 1951. For the next eighteen years, the comic story robot hero _____ (9. entertain) the Japanese audience. In 1963, this incredibly popular robot _____ (10. star) in Japan's first animated TV series. Unlike his Western counterparts, P-2 _____ (11. not look) menacing at all. He had huge eyes and spiky hair, and indeed he appeared benign and friendly. He _____ (12. help) the world by fighting monsters and criminals.

Perhaps this positive portrayal explains why a lot of time and money are spent on robotic research in Japan. Many people _____ a real role for robots
13. (see)
in Japan in the future. For example, robots may be able to help take care of the increasing number of elderly people who will require care. By early in the next century, Japan's older population _____ tremendously: At that time, one in four Japanese people
14. (increase)
_____ over sixty-five. Perhaps a robot _____ able to help
15. (be)   16. (be)
these elders to walk and sit and stand, to eat and to exercise, and it _____
17. (dispense)
their medication for them.

Many researchers firmly _____ that in the next century robots will
18. (believe)
be everywhere. It is not a question of *if* but rather *when* robots _____
19. (perform)
many of the mundane, boring tasks that humans now do. By 2100, perhaps, personal robots _____ such tedious tasks as raking leaves, shoveling snow, washing
20. (take over)
windows, and arranging papers. This idea may seem far-fetched at this moment in time; however, the computers and e-mail that we use on a daily basis _____
21. (seem)
like a far-fetched idea, too.*

*Adapted from Bob Johnstone, "Japan's Friendly Robots" (www.techreview.com:80/articles/may99/johnstone.htm).

3 USING VERB TENSES

The following is the text of a commencement speech, made by Professor J. Henry Bright, at South State University last Friday. Select the correct verb form in parentheses for each blank space.

Good afternoon, ladies and gentlemen:

We are gathered here today to celebrate a commencement, not just an ending of this phase of your studies. True, your studies at this level _____have ended_____: You
1. (have ended / had ended)

_____ your academic programs. Congratulations! And now
2. (have finished / were finishing)

consider the word *commencement*. "To commence" _____ "to
3. (means / is meaning)

begin," and now you _____ on the beginning of the rest of your
4. (are embarking / embark)

lives.

At this time last year, what _____? You
5. (did you do / were you doing)

_____ your semester examinations, and you
6. (have just finished / had just finished)

_____ a bit before starting a summer trip or job. You
7. (probably relaxed / were probably relaxing)

_____ forward to the end of your college studies.
8. (were probably looking / have probably been looking)

Look how far you _____ in just one year!
9. (had gone / have gone)

And a year from now, what do you think _____? Some of you
10. (you will do / you'll be doing)

will be in school again, studying for a more advanced degree. Many of you _____ **11. (will have worked / will be working)** in your chosen areas and will feel far away from the carefree days of college. But all of you _____ **12. (will remember / will have remembered)** your days here at South State University. You'll remember your professors, your friends, your classes; all of you _____ **13. (will have benefited / would benefit)** greatly from your years here at one of the greatest academic institutions in the world.

I know of a woman who _____ **14. (was beginning / began)** college rather late in life—at age forty-five. Before this time, she _____ **15. (had been raising / has raised)** a family and working as a secretary in an accountant's office at the same time. While she _____, **16. (worked / was working)** her boss, the accountant, noticed what a quick and eager mind she _____, **17. (was possessing / possessed)** and he encouraged her to apply to the university and finally to attend. At first, she resisted the idea. She _____ **18. (had been working / was working)** all day long and _____ **19. (had been / used to be)** so tired at night that she _____ **20. (would fall / was falling)** into bed right after dinner. She couldn't imagine an additional commitment, and she _____ **21. (thought / was thinking)** she _____ **22. (will have to / would have to)** continue working to support herself and her family. But the accountant found a scholarship for her and also persuaded her parents to help out with expenses at home. She _____ **23. (has gotten / got)** her degree two years ago, second in her class of 2,400. Last year she entered an M.B.A. program, and she _____ **24. (is graduating / has graduated)** next February. She already _____ **25. (has / will have)** a job in a top accounting firm—beginning right after she _____ **26. (will graduate / graduates)** — at twice the salary she _____ **27. (used to make / has made)** as a secretary. By the time she _____ **28. (gets / will get)** her degree, she _____ **29. (will have been studying / will be studying)** for six years. More important, she _____ **30. (will have succeeded / will have been succeeding)** in obtaining something wonderful: the realization of her goals despite difficult circumstances.

When you _____ **31. (are / will be)** forty-five, you too _____ **32. (have had / will have)** opportunities to continue to improve yourselves. Take

(continued on next page)

advantage of those opportunities! Keep the spirit of accomplishment alive, and keep on accomplishing. You _____ the academic
33. (have successfully completed / were successfully completing)
program at South State University, one of many goals that you _____
34. (are reaching / will reach)
in your lives.

Congratulations, graduates!

4 USING VERB TENSES

This conversation occurred at a high school reunion that took place ten years after graduation. Circle the letter of the phrase or phrases to complete the sentences correctly.

A: Al Albert

B: Bob Bradley

1. **A:** Hi, Bob! Great to see you!

   B: Great to see you, too, Al. What _____ for these past ten years?

      a. did you do   **(c.)** have you been doing

      b. have you done   **d.** had you done

2. **A:** Well, I _____ medical training. I _____ my first job on my

   own as a doctor in two weeks, on July 1.

      a. had just finished / start   **c.** just finish / 've started

      b. 've just finished / 'm starting   **d.** will just finish / started

3. **B:** Oh, so you're a doctor. I thought you _____ law.

      a. study   **c.** are studying

      b. have studied   **d.** were studying

4. **A:** You have a good memory. I _____ law, but I decided to go into medicine

   instead.

      a. studied   **c.** would study

      b. have studied   **d.** was going to study

5. **A:** What about you?

   B: I write television scripts. That is, I write them, but I _____ them. So far, I _____ only one.

   a. don't sell / 've sold
   b. didn't sell / 've been selling
   c. hadn't sold / had sold
   d. won't sell / sell

6. **A:** Well, it takes time to succeed in the TV business. I remember that you _____ the funniest guy in our class. Whenever you made a joke, everybody _____ laugh so much.

   a. had been / used to
   b. used to be / would
   c. would be / used to
   d. have been / was laughing

7. **B:** As a matter of fact, I _____ comedy. I just hope that one day an important producer _____ one of the forty-seven scripts I've written.

   a. have been writing / will like
   b. had been writing / would like
   c. will write / will like
   d. have written / liked

8. **A:** Don't give up! A producer _____ one of your scripts soon, I'm sure.

   a. is picking up
   b. picks up
   c. will pick up
   d. would pick up

9. **A:** Remember Jenny Lee? She wrote a novel that eleven publishers _____, and then just last week Brown-Smith Publishing _____ it.

   a. were rejecting / was accepting
   b. have rejected / has accepted
   c. rejected / accepted
   d. had rejected / was accepting

   B: I'm sure she's delighted.

10. **A:** Of course. Now, tell me about you and Rose. Do you have any children?

    B: Oh, Rose and I _____ married only for two years. _____ married to Melissa for the past five years.

    a. have been / I've been
    b. were / I was
    c. used to be / I'm
    d. were / I've been

11. **A:** You _____ divorced from Rose? You and Rose, the class sweethearts? I'm sorry.

    a. get
    b. got
    c. were getting
    d. had been getting

    B: It's OK. We're both better off. You would like Melissa. She's in medical school, by the way.

12. **A:** Really? What field _____ into?

    a. does she go
    b. is she going
    c. will she have gone
    d. would she go

    B: Pediatrics.

    A: What a coincidence! That's my field, too.

    B: Great! Let's all have dinner together at our house. We can talk about our professional futures and our not-so-professional pasts.

13. **A:** Right. Our carefree pasts. Do you remember how our biggest concern _____ whether or not we _____ a date on Saturday night?

    a. had been / used to have
    b. used to be / would have
    c. would be / used to have
    d. was / have had

14. **B:** I sure do. Those were the good old days. At our *fiftieth* reunion, _____ that these are the good old days!

    a. we say
    b. we'll have said
    c. we'll have been saying
    d. we'll be saying

5 USING VERB TENSES

The murder trial of Jesse Jones is being broadcast live on TV. Because of technical difficulties, some of the verbs cannot be heard. Complete the sentences with the correct form of the verbs in parentheses. More than one form may be possible.

We are here in the Washington County Courthouse at the trial of Jesse Jones, who is accused of murdering his wife. We __are now waiting__ for today's session to begin. As you
                          1. (wait / now)

know, Jones has pleaded innocent to this horrendous charge. Today we _____
                                                              2. (hear)

the testimony of his mother, who will probably claim that Jesse always _____ a
                                                                    3. (be)

good little boy and that he _____ her every day since the day fifteen years ago
                                  4. (telephone)

when he _____ home. Yesterday, you remember, Jesse Jones's fifth-grade teacher
              5. (leave)

_____ quite a different story; she _____ that when Jesse was in her
6. (tell)   **7. (testify)**

class, he _____ the other children's pencils and money all the time.
       8. (steal)

This morning we heard the testimony of Jones's good friend, Harry Bliss, who

_____ that he and Jones _____ to play tennis together at 7:00 P.M. on
9. (state)   **10. (go)**

August 21, the night of the murder. They _____ for about half an hour, he said,
                                              11. (play)

when they _____ in the middle of a game because Harry's bad knee
            12. (stop)

_____ him again. They then drove to a nearby fast-food place for a hamburger
13. (hurt)

before going to Jesse Jones's home, where they _____ his wife dead on the floor
                                                          14. (find)

at about 8:30 P.M.

(continued on next page)

Unit 3

This is in direct contrast to the testimony of a neighbor of the Joneses, who said that he _____ Jesse Jones and his wife, Madelaine, together at 8:00 P.M. At that time,
15. (see)

from about 7:50 to 8:05, Jesse and Madelaine Jones _____ very loud, possibly
16. (talk)

even having an argument, the neighbor said. Then they both _____ into the
17. (go)

house.

Now, here comes the judge, the Honorable Sheldon O'Malley. We _____
18. (wait)

expectantly for more than an hour for his appearance! In a few minutes, today's session of

the trial will commence. Oh, what's that? The judge _____ something now.
19. (say)

Ladies and gentlemen, it now _____ that today's session of this trial could be
20. (seem)

postponed. Yes, the judge has just said that the trial _____ tomorrow at 9:00
21. (continue)

A.M. The defendant's lawyer _____ one extra day to call a very important witness
22. (request)

to the stand. He says that this witness _____ the innocence of his client. Stay
23. (prove)

tuned, ladies and gentlemen.

Tomorrow at this time, I know that you _____ the mystery witness on this
24. (watch)

channel, when he—or she—speaks from the witness stand. By the end of the day

tomorrow, I think that we _____ where Jesse Jones *really* was on the night of
25. (learn / already)

August 21.

6 EDITING

Read this student's letter to a friend. What kinds of problems is Marco having? What new things has he encountered? Find and correct the twenty errors in verb tense usage.

Dear Ricardo,

                                                      is

How are things going there? I hope everything ~~was~~ O.K. with you and your family. I'm missing everybody at home very much.

I am here in the United States for about three weeks now. I don't think I do very well in my English classes right now, and the teachers give too much homework. In fact, we have homework every night since the course began. Maybe the work load gets lighter soon. I certainly hope so.

Life here is very different from life at home. Everyone here is always in a hurry. People are different, too. They aren't seeming so friendly, and I being lonely. I have been thinking about my family and friends a lot these past few days.

Some of the customs here are strange to me, like meals. First, all the food is tasting the same; it doesn't has much flavor. Then, people are eating dinner so early. I live in the dorm, and I have paid for my meals already, so I have to eat in the school cafeteria. They're serving dinner every day at the cafeteria from 5:00 until 7:00 P.M. Can you imagine! At those hours, I often think of all of you at home, and I wonder what you do: probably you work or maybe you enjoy a little aperitif with some friends. Back home, nobody is having dinner before 8:00 P.M.!

Another thing that is different here is that people use machines all the time. For example, they're having huge machines that wash their cars. And, they have filled up their own cars with gas, which they pay for simply by inserting their credit cards into a slot in the gas pump. They never are needing to talk to an attendant! Many times I have wanted to talk to a human being.

By the time you get this letter, I have been here a whole month. I have survived so far, and I suppose that I will continue to do so, in spite of the cultural differences I'm experiencing. Please write soon.

Your friend,

Marco

7 PERSONALIZATION

Write a short essay about a person who has influenced your life. Tell about the ways he or she has influenced you. Use as many of the phrases in the box as possible.

> I first met . . .
> I knew right away . . .
> He (She) always knew . . .
> We have always had . . .
> When I went away, . . .
> We hadn't seen each other for a long time when . . .
> Since that time, . . .
> We see each other every . . .
> By the time I see him (her) again, . . .
> I will always remember . . .

PART II MODALS

UNIT 4

MODALS: NECESSITY

1 USING MODAL EXPRESSIONS OF NECESSITY

The following is information provided by The FitNiche, a place where people go to become healthier and stronger. Complete the passage by selecting the correct modal in parentheses for each of the blank spaces.

THE FITNICHE

People who want to benefit from our program ___must not___
                                              1. (must not / don't have to)
eat junk food. In order to benefit, they _____
                                         2. (should / might)
eat only the food prescribed by The FitNiche. This food is tasty; contrary

to what many people think, healthy food _____
                                         3. (doesn't have to / must not)
taste terrible. We think that our participants _____
                                                4. (should / had better)
take a vitamin–mineral supplement, too, to ensure getting all the necessary

nutrition; however, people who are sure they are eating properly

_____ take supplements.
 5. (don't have to / must not)

The program has certain rules about exercise: participants

_____ exercise at least three times a week and
 6. (have to / should)
_____ exercise for at least 30 minutes each
 7. (must / could)
time. In fact, participants _____ exercise five
                             8. (should / had better)
times a week if possible, even though this is not a program requirement.

In addition, The FitNiche offers yoga, meditation, tai chi, and life

coaching for those who want the benefits from such disciplines. There is

(continued on next page)

no extra charge for these activities, and if you want to try them, you _____.
9. (ought to / had better)

Finally, all members are closely monitored by our professional staff. We speak with you each time that you come, in order to find out how you are progressing in the program. If you _____ exercise and you didn't have the time, we'll counsel
10. (had to / were supposed to)
you about making changes in your schedule.

Remember that The FitNiche wants you to be healthy and to enjoy getting healthy. At the end of our program, you will say: "I _____ change my
11. (had to / was supposed to)
habits, but it wasn't difficult at all. Now I'm going to stay healthy, thanks to The FitNiche. I _____ come here much sooner."
12. (should have / had better)

2 USING MODAL EXPRESSIONS OF NECESSITY

The following are dialogues that take place between a teacher and her class. Some of the students are often late or absent from class. Circle the letter of the verb phrase to complete each sentence correctly.

1. "Why didn't you come to class yesterday, Barbara?"

   "Oh, I'm so sorry, Ms. Smith. I couldn't come to class because I _____ to the doctor. I was sick."

   a. should have gone   **b.** was supposed to go   **(c.)** had to go

2. "Why didn't you come to class yesterday, Nicole?"

   "Oh, I'm so sorry, Ms. Smith. My husband _____ me here as usual, but he couldn't get out of bed. He was very sick."

   a. drove   **b.** was supposed to drive   **c.** had to drive

3. "What about you, Edward? Why didn't you come to class yesterday?"

   "Oh, I'm so sorry, Ms. Smith. I overslept. I _____ up earlier."

   a. had to get   **b.** should have gotten   **c.** got

Modals: Necessity   33

4. "Philip, why weren't you in class yesterday?"

   "Oh, but I _____ in class yesterday, Ms. Smith. I was sitting right here! Don't you remember?"

   a. should have been   **b.** had to be   **c.** was

5. "Why didn't you come to your first class this morning, Kevin?"

   "Oh, I'm sorry, Ms. Smith. I _____ to school at 9:25, but I didn't want to interrupt the class so I didn't enter."

   a. had to get   **b.** should have gotten   **c.** got

6. "Why isn't Sara in class today?"

   "She _____ to do an important errand. She told us yesterday that she was planning to do that today."

   a. should have gone   **b.** could go   **c.** had to go

7. "Martin, you missed a very important class yesterday."

   "I know, Ms. Smith. I _____, but I didn't feel well so I stayed in bed all day."

   a. should have come   **b.** had to come   **c.** came

8. "David, you'll be first tomorrow to give your presentation."

   "Oh, Ms. Smith, _____ to my consulate tomorrow. I can't come to class!"

   a. I should go   **b.** I've got to go   **c.** I could go

9. "Students, you all did well on the last test, except for using the verb tenses correctly. You _____ learn those verb tenses! It's a necessity!"

   a. should   **b.** must   **c.** are supposed to

10. "Students, this material that we've been covering is very important. _____ miss any classes this week, or you will not do well on your final exam."

    a. You'd better not   **b.** You don't have to   **c.** You're not supposed to

34 Unit 4

3 USING MODAL EXPRESSIONS OF NECESSITY

Lucia receives comments from Amanda about the ad she is going to place in the Personals section. Complete Amanda's e-mail with the verb phrases from the box. Use each item once.

can list	could invent	got to meet	has to catch
have to give	might be	might say	~~have to give~~
must write	should continue	should make	should say

Dear Lucia:

Your ad is OK, but I don't think it's attractive enough. You ___have to give___ it
1.
interest and vitality. You need to make yourself appear irresistible.

First of all, you _____ an interesting "hook." That means the
2.
first phrase _____ the casual reader like a fish hook. You
3.
_____ something like "High school prom queen, now a corporate
4.
lawyer."

Then you _____ by listing the qualities you find attractive in a
5.
man. You _____ "seeks educated, cosmopolitan gentleman who's
6.
kind, playful, and witty." Or you _____ a mythical setting and say
7.
"Fairy princess seeks Prince Charming."

After that, you _____ your assets. Choose adjectives that indicate
8.
that you are beautiful, smart, and nice.

Finally, write an ending that completely entices the reader. It _____
9.
him think: "I've _____ this person. She really _____
10. 11.
Ms. Right for me!"

I like what you have written. It's a good beginning. However, if you can make just a

few small changes, I'll bet you'll soon find someone right for you.

Love,

Amanda

4 USING MODAL EXPRESSIONS OF NECESSITY

In the weekly advice column of the daily newspaper, "Dear Doctor" answers questions from readers. In this column, someone is seeking advice on how to find time to exercise. Fill in the blanks with one of the words or expressions from the box above each section.

> ~~am I supposed to~~   can   can't   should

Dear Doctor:

Where __am I supposed to__ find the time to exercise? I know I _____
                    1.   **2.**

exercise, but I really _____ fit it into my busy day. What's more, I hate
                                3.

jumping around and lifting weights and all that stuff. Is there something I

_____ do instead of going to the gym?
    4.

                                                                                                        Discouraged

> can   don't have to   must   should   shouldn't

Dear Discouraged:

There's good news for you! You _____ do all those activities that are
                                                  5.

so unpleasant for you. Instead, you _____ get many of the same health
                                                         6.

benefits just by being more active in your daily routine.

For example, instead of parking near the supermarket or the front door of an office

building, you _____ choose a spot at the far end of the parking lot.
               7.

(continued on next page)

Unit 4

You _____8._____ take the elevator to go up a few floors; you _____9._____ walk up instead. In place of public transportation in your own city, you _____10._____ walk to as many places as you can. Taking just these few suggestions will give you quite a bit of extra activity.

Recent research has shown that by taking this more active approach to daily living, you _____11._____ avoid weight gain even if you consume the same number of calories. If you use up only 100 calories less per day and eat the same amount as usual, you will gain 10 pounds a year. So you _____12._____ be on a strict diet, but you _____13._____ be active. Being active is the key.

> might OR could   should   have to   better not

Try some of these different ways of adding activity to your ordinary life. At the office, you _____14._____ walk over to your colleague's office to discuss something instead of e-mailing him. Or, you _____15._____ walk a half-mile to a restaurant instead of driving. You _____16._____ try bicycling to work instead of driving. At home and on weekends, you _____17._____ do gardening, or wash your car, or polish furniture, or saw wood by hand, or rake leaves, or even sweep or mop the floor.

Wherever you are, you _____18._____ always keep this in mind: I'd _____19._____ let the fat creep up on me!

Yours in good health,

Harry Healthmore, M.D.

5 USING MODAL EXPRESSIONS OF NECESSITY

When you are invited to someone's home for dinner, do you take a gift? If so, what kind of gift is appropriate? Read this story of a Japanese student who faced this dilemma when he was in the United States. Fill in the blanks with the correct modal expressions.

are supposed to say	~~must take~~
could find	should have brought
could have been	should I have bought
could have learned	should I buy
could have brought	was supposed to do
didn't have to bring	have to pay
had better be	will have to come

WHAT'S THE RIGHT THING TO DO?

Tetsuya is a Japanese student who has been studying English in the United States for about six months. Last Saturday he went to the home of one of his American friends, Jason, who had invited Tetsuya to have dinner with him and his family.

Since this was Tetsuya's first dinner with an American family, he was a little nervous. He thought to himself, "As a guest, I ____must take____ a gift to the family, as we do in
                                                         1.
Japan. What _____?" he wondered. He decided to buy a watermelon, a
                    2.
very desirable and prestigious gift in Japan.

He chose the most delicious-looking watermelon that he _____. To
                                                                    3.
Tetsuya, American watermelons seemed big—much bigger than Japanese watermelons, which are round, not long and oval as they are in the United States. In Japan, watermelons are quite expensive; you _____ $15 to $20 for a nice one.
                                    4.

He took his watermelon home and placed it in a nice box, which he then wrapped with pretty paper. He left his apartment at 5:30, carrying his heavy gift. As he walked to Jason's house and his arm began to hurt, he began to wonder about the watermelon.

"_____ the watermelon?" he thought to himself.
         5.

Tetsuya arrived at Jason's house at 7 o'clock sharp. Jason had told him, "My mom is a very punctual person who doesn't like late people, so you _____ on time
                                                                              6.

(continued on next page)

at 7:00, or she'll get angry!" Of course, Jason was just joking, but he wanted Tetsuya to arrive as close to 7:00 as possible.

When Tetsuya arrived at Jason's home, he was welcomed graciously and he gave the beautifully wrapped watermelon to Jason's mother. Jason's mother opened the box and said, "Oh, isn't this—um—interesting . . . a watermelon. What a nice gift! Well, Tetsuya! You _____7._____ anything, but we do thank you very much for your gift." Actually, she didn't know what she _____8._____ do with the watermelon. She had already prepared a lovely dessert, and besides, there was no time to chill the watermelon.

Tetsuya quickly replied, "It's just a small uninteresting gift," which is a translation of a Japanese expression that you _____9._____ whenever you give a gift to someone. Jason's mother smiled at Tetsuya and put the watermelon in the kitchen. "We'll enjoy this tomorrow," she said politely. "You _____10._____ back to eat it with us."

Tetsuya now realizes that the watermelon was not a very good gift idea because watermelons are not considered special in the United States. He still doesn't know, however, what sort of gift he _____11._____ instead. However, it really didn't matter. The evening was a great success. Jason's family was most hospitable, and Tetsuya was most appreciative. Perhaps Tetsuya _____12._____ something else, and perhaps Jason's family _____13._____ more about Japanese customs beforehand, but the warmth and good feelings that were exchanged were more valuable than any material gift _____14._____.

6 EDITING

*Read this story by an English teacher. There are eleven underlined phrases—in addition to the two examples—using modals. If the underlined part is wrong, write the correction above it. If it is correct, write **C** above it.*

      This is a true story about one of my students, Ana. I <u>can to</u> [can't] remember the first day she came to my class: She <u>couldn't</u> [C] speak any English at all. She spoke only Spanish.

      One time during the holidays between school terms, the dorms were closed, so the students <u>have to find</u> a place to live during the break. Ana stayed with an American host family, and after the vacation, she asked me what she <u>might to do</u> to thank her new friends for their hospitality. "Well, you <u>could send</u> them a gift," I told her. "Or you <u>must just send</u> them a nice card."

      Ana decided that she <u>will send</u> a card. She asked, "<u>Am I supposed to get</u> a separate card for each member of the family?"

      "No, you <u>haven't to do</u> that. What you <u>ought to do</u> is get a nice card for the family and write a thoughtful message inside."

      "But my English is not so good," she protested.

      "Ok, bring me the card and I'll help you write your message," I offered.

      Ana was extremely busy and <u>could easily have forgotten</u> her good intentions, but she didn't. The next day after class, she showed me a beautiful card. On the front of it were the words: "In sympathy." On the inside were the words: "You have my deepest sympathy. You are in my thoughts at this time."

      But, there was a big mistake! The card that Ana had bought was a sympathy card, a card that you send when someone has died. Ana had confused the Spanish word "simpatico," which translates to 'nice' in English, with the English word "sympathetic," which expresses the emotions of feeling sorry about someone's death.

      When Ana realized her mistake, she had a good long laugh. She said that she <u>must have asked</u> someone to help her pick out the right card. Now Ana's English is excellent, and she <u>must not have</u> any help any more.

7 PERSONALIZATION

Life presents us with many opportunities to do different things. Sometimes we take advantage of an opportunity: we choose to do something new or different. Sometimes we miss an opportunity: we don't do it. Think about a time when you missed an opportunity, when you had a chance to do something but you didn't. What was the opportunity? Why didn't you choose to do it?

Are you happy or sad that you didn't? What did you learn from the experience? Write a short essay beginning with this sentence: "One opportunity in my life that I missed was . . ." In your essay include some of the phrases in the box.

> I shouldn't have . . .
> Instead, I should have . . .
> I could/might have . . .
> I didn't realize that I was supposed to . . .
> Because of that missed opportunity, I had to . . .
> In the future, I have to . . .
> In the future, I should . . .
> I have learned that I'd better . . .

UNIT 5

MODALS: CERTAINTY

1 USING MODAL EXPRESSIONS OF CERTAINTY

The following are the visible first lines of stories on the Internet. What can you conclude about the next information in each one? Select a phrase from this list to complete each sentence.

be very angry	be very effective	~~have been bad~~	have snowed recently
like skiing	be operative	be in jail	want to anger the voters
have cheated	speak Japanese	have won a big victory	

1. Food Poisoning at Seafood Heaven. Forty-six people who ate the shrimp at Seafood Heaven, a restaurant on the western shore, last Thursday night became ill with food poisoning. Other people who ate at the restaurant were unaffected.

   The shrimp must _____have been bad_____.

2. 34% of Students Admit Cheating. Thirty-four percent of college students admit they have cheated on tests or on written work during their academic career. An example of an otherwise honest person is Henry S., who . . .

   Henry S. must _____.

3. Scam Impoverishes Senior Citizens. An illegal operation, run by three con men in Minnesota, succeeded in taking hundreds of thousands of dollars from several elders in small towns in that state. In many cases, the money was the life savings of . . .

   These senior citizens must _____.

   The three con men now must _____.

(continued on next page)

4. <u>Hurricane Lashes Coast</u>. Winds of 120 miles per hour, and tides as high as 10 feet, whipped the shores of North Carolina early this morning. We cannot confirm, but it is believed . . .

   Communications in the storm area must not _____.

5. <u>Heavy Response to Request to House Foreign Tennis Players</u>. Sixteen students from various countries arrived in Springfield today for the annual College Tennis Championships. A call had gone out especially for hosts who can speak Japanese, and eight households responded with offers of hospitality for . . .

   The people in these households must _____.

6. <u>New Anti-Headache Medicine</u>. A new medication used to treat severe and frequent headaches has relieved symptoms dramatically in 86% of patients . . .

   The new medication must _____.

7. <u>Congress at a Standstill</u>. A proposal to enact new legislation to raise income taxes has not gone very far in the House of Representatives. Although everyone agrees that more money is necessary to run government programs, very few legislators want to go on record as . . .

   The legislators must not _____.

8. <u>Pennsylvania Players Celebrate in Philadelphia</u>. The Pennsylvania Men's Soccer Team came home to a wild celebration in downtown Philadelphia yesterday. Pictured are . . .

   The soccer team from Pennsylvania must _____.

9. <u>Unseasonable Heat in Europe</u>. An unseasonable heat wave lingers in Switzerland, Italy, Austria, and France, causing the cancellation of thousands of bookings for the Christmas ski season and . . .

   The people who canceled must _____.

   It must not _____.

2 USING MODAL EXPRESSIONS OF CERTAINTY

*Can you answer the following questions? Using the **HINT** below the question, write the correct modal auxiliary in one blank space; wherever possible, write the correct geographical answer in the other blank.*

INTERESTING WORLD FACTS

1. The longest river in the world is

   a. the Nile.   **b.** the Mississippi.   **c.** the Danube.

   HINT: The river is in Africa, so it ___has to___ be ___the Nile___.
   (might / has to)

2. The highest waterfalls in the world are

   a. Niagara Falls.   **b.** Victoria Falls.   **c.** Angel Falls.

   HINT: The falls are in South America, so the answer _____ be
   (must not / can't)
   Niagara Falls.

3. The highest mountain in the world is Mt. Everest. It's located in

   a. India.   **b.** Turkey.   **c.** Nepal and Tibet.

   HINT: Turkey does not have extremely high mountains, so the answer

   _____ be India, or it _____ be Nepal and Tibet.
   (might / must)   (might / must)

4. At the millennium, the most highly populated cities in the world were

   a. Seoul, Tokyo, and   **b.** New York, Toronto, and   **c.** Bombay, São Paolo, and
   Mexico City.   London.   Paris.

   HINT: The correct answer does not include a European city, so the answer

   _____ be _____.
   (might / must)

5. At the millennium, the country with the largest land area is

   a. Russia.   **b.** Canada.   **c.** Brazil.

   HINT: The country has, mostly, a cold climate, and it is in the Northern Hemisphere.

   It _____ be Russia, or it _____ be Canada.
   (could / should)   (could / should)

(continued on next page)

6. At the end of the twentieth century, the country with the largest population was

   a. China.   **b.** India.   **c.** the United States of America.

   HINT: This country's capital is Beijing. According to projections from the U.S. Bureau of the Census, in 2028 this country _____ no longer have the
   (must / should)
   largest population in the world because of its strong efforts to limit the size of its families. The answer is _____.

7. At the end of the twentieth century, the country with the most cellular telephones per person was

   a. the United States.   **b.** the United Kingdom.   **c.** Norway.

   HINT: This country is in Scandinavia. The people in this country _____ talk on the phone a lot! It's _____.
   (must / might)

8. At the end of the millennium, the people in this country were attending live theater performances more frequently than those in any other country:

   a. France.   **b.** Japan.   **c.** Cuba.

   HINT: The people in this country speak Spanish, so the answer _____ be _____.
   (could / has to)

9. This country has played the most soccer games in the final stages of the World Cup:

   a. Brazil.   **b.** Argentina.   **c.** Italy.

   HINT: The people in this country don't speak Spanish, so it _____
   (might / should)
   be Brazil, or it _____ be Italy.
   (might / should)

10. The country where they drink the most coffee per person is

   a. Guatemala.   **b.** Finland.   **c.** Egypt.

   HINT: In this country, they _____ drink a lot of coffee—1,581 cups
   (can / must)
   per year per person—in order to keep warm! It's _____.

*Source of all questions: *The Top Ten of Everything* (New York, New York: DK Publishing, 1999).

3 USING MODAL EXPRESSIONS OF CERTAINTY

Two of the teachers at the Intensive English Language Program at Montgomery Community College are talking about their students. The program has three levels of English: one beginning class, two intermediate classes, and six advanced classes. Using the information in the chart, underline the correct modal in the sentences that follow.

STUDENT NAME	COUNTRY	CLASS	EMPLOYMENT GOAL
Beyhan Nurev	Turkey	Intermediate	to be an accountant
Hiba Rashid	Jordan	Beginner	to work in an international bank
Jared Larson	Sweden	Beginner	to be a chemical engineer
Jenny Chan	Singapore	Advanced	to teach English in Singapore
Mario Rivas	Mexico	Intermediate	to be a computer engineer
Roberto Beltran	Colombia	Advanced	to work in public relations for an international company

1. Some of the students have cars. Beyhan (must / <u>might</u>) have a car, but I'm not sure.
2. Mario (might / must) speak English better than Jared.
3. Jenny (might / must) be older than Hiba.
4. Jared (might / must) know Hiba.
5. Roberto (could / couldn't) know Mario.
6. Jenny speaks English and Chinese. Hiba speaks Arabic and English. They had lunch together yesterday. They (could / must) have spoken to each other in English.
7. Mario (may / must) have traveled to France and England.
8. Jenny is only eighteen years old. She (must / could) not have taught English in a high school.
9. Mario (might / must) know something about computers already.
10. Beyhan (might / must) be interested in numbers.
11. Jared (might / must) have seen snow.
12. Mario isn't very happy at this school. He thinks that it (might / might not) have been a mistake to attend this college.
13. Jenny and Roberto are both advanced students, but they (may / may not) be in the same class.
14. Hiba and Roberto (can't / might not) be in the same class.
15. Beyhan failed the last test, but all of the other students passed it. Beyhan admits that the test was actually quite easy. She (must / must not) have studied very much.
16. Jared is really interested in chemistry. Both his parents are chemists. He is a hard worker. He (should / must) be very successful in this field in the future.

4 COMPARING MODAL EXPRESSIONS OF CERTAINTY

Two students at Montgomery Community College are conversing. For each item below, circle the letter of the choice that is similar in meaning to the original sentence.

1. If you need help with grammar, ask Ms. Jones. She should be able to help you.
   a. Ms. Jones may be able to help you.
   (b.) Ms. Jones can probably help you.
2. If you're looking for authentic Thai food ingredients, you might go to that small store on 56th Street.
   a. That store could have what you are looking for.
   b. That store must have what you are looking for.
3. Mr. McKenna has got to be at least fifty years old.
   a. The speaker is almost certain that Mr. McKenna is fifty or older.
   b. The speaker doesn't think that Mr. McKenna is fifty yet.
4. Juan said he missed eight questions on the test. The test had only seven questions.
   a. Juan might have failed the test.
   b. Juan couldn't have missed eight questions.
5. Ben is an upper-level manager. His office is open for business from 9 to 5. It is now 6:10 P.M.
   a. He must not be in the office now.
   b. He should not be at the office now.
6. Ben works from 9 to 5. It's 6:30 now.
   a. He might be at home.
   b. He must be at home.
7. Class begins at 10:00. It's 9:55, but the teacher is not in the room now. The teacher is not ill, and nothing unusual has happened.
   a. She may be here soon.
   b. She should be here soon.
8. The soccer game was called off. Franco showed up for the game anyway.
   a. He must not have heard about the cancellation.
   b. He could not have heard about the cancellation.
9. Peter is a great cook. We're going to eat dinner at his house tomorrow night.
   a. The food tomorrow night must be delicious.
   b. The food tomorrow night should be delicious.
10. I need to buy a new dictionary. A good dictionary should cost about $20.
    a. The speaker is sure that the price will be $20.
    b. The speaker expects to pay about $20.

5 USING MODAL EXPRESSIONS

Three friends have just arrived at a restaurant, and they are talking about their choices. Use the modals and verbs in the box to complete their pre-dinner conversation.

can still do	could have eaten	could have ordered	couldn't eat	might make
~~must have~~	must be (3 times)	ought to be / should be (2 times)	should take	

NANCY: I wonder if they serve cheeseburgers here. I don't see it on the menu.

BILL: I saw a poster with all sorts of sandwiches on it by the door, so I'm sure they _____must have_____ cheeseburgers. Keep looking. It _____ on the menu somewhere.
         1.   2.

SHARON: Wow, listen to this. They have a sandwich that has roast chicken, roast beef, and cheese. It's covered with a special mayonnaise sauce. Doesn't that sound great?

BILL: Are you kidding? I _____ that. Do you know how unhealthy
                                    3.
that sandwich is? Do you realize how fattening that _____?
                                                                  4.

SHARON: Well, I don't care. It _____ me fat, but it won't kill
                                5.
me. And it sounds delicious. Nancy, what are you going to have?

NANCY: Well, I'm not that hungry, so I'm looking for something that's not too filling. What about this vegetable snack plate?

BILL: Hmm . . . yes, that _____ light. Why don't you get that?
                                              6.

NANCY: I've never ordered that here before. It sounds like it _____ perfect.
                                                                   7.

BILL: I feel like eating barbecue, but they don't have that here.

SHARON: We drove past Bob's Barbecue when we came here. We _____ there. You should have said something!
                                                                                           8.

BILL: You're right. I forgot about that place. Let's go there.

(continued on next page)

NANCY: When? You mean now?

BILL: Yeah, sure. We haven't ordered yet, so we _____ that.
9.

NANCY: You _____ crazy! I'm not getting up and leaving a
10.
restaurant. How embarrassing!

SHARON: It's too late, because here comes the waitress.

WAITRESS: Hi, are you folks ready to order?

NANCY: I'll have the vegetable snack plate. And I'd like iced tea, please.

SHARON: I'd like the beef, chicken, and cheese sandwich, please. And bring me iced tea as well.

BILL: I'll have a roast chicken sandwich and iced tea to drink.

WAITRESS: Ok, we're not too busy right now, so your orders _____ only
11.
about 10 minutes. I'll be right back with your drinks.

(The waitress leaves.)

SHARON: Hey, Bill, look at that sign. It says they have a barbecued beef sandwich.

BILL: Oh, no. I didn't see it! So I _____ barbecue after all.
12.

6 USING MODAL EXPRESSIONS OF CERTAINTY

Read the information and tell whether the sentences following it are **True** *or* **False**. *Then write a short explanation for each answer.*

> There was a murder at the Nelsons' house last night. Mr. Nelson, a very wealthy eighty-year-old man, was murdered. The police are investigating, and they believe someone in the house was the murderer. The murder happened at about 10 P.M. The police found the body in the living room. The police are sure only one person committed this crime.
>
> PERSONS IN THE NELSONS' HOUSE:
>
> | | | |
> |---|---|---|
> | Mildred | wife | She is old and walks with a cane. She went to bed at 9:30 P.M. |
> | Belinda | cousin | She is forty-five years old. She was envious of the family's wealth. |
> | Mark | cousin | He is Belinda's husband. He didn't come home until 11 P.M. |
> | Georgia | niece | She is Belinda and Mark's baby. She is only two years old. |
> | Frank | brother | Frank is visiting from New York. He loved his brother very much and is sincerely upset over this matter. |
> | Karla | the maid | Karla has been with the Nelsons for over thirty years. She usually goes to bed at 10 P.M., but last night she was awake in her room until midnight. |

_____True_____ 1. Karla could have heard the murder.
   She was awake at the time.

_____ 2. Georgia could have killed her uncle.

_____ 3. The murderer might have used a knife to kill Mr. Nelson.

_____ 4. Belinda might have killed Mr. Nelson.

_____ 5. Mildred must have killed her husband.

_____ 6. Frank must not have been the killer.

_____ 7. The killer must have shot Mr. Nelson with a gun.

_____ 8. Mr. Nelson must have had more money than his cousin Belinda.

7 EDITING

Ricardo answers his friend Marco's e-mail. In the e-mail, there are six errors in the use of modals of certainty. There are also some modals of certainty that are correct. Find the six errors and correct them.

From: Ricardo T.
To: Marco F.
Subject: Problems

Dear Marco:

   I guess you must not to be so happy over there. That's too bad. I'm going to give you a pep talk: Things have got get better soon because it looks like, in your case, you think they can't getting worse. Be realistic! Don't expect that things are going to be good all the time. You have to go out and socialize with people. They might not be so friendly at first, but after you smile and are nice, everybody should have liked you.

   You think you've got problems? Last week Emilia left me, right after I got fired. That's right. I lost my job. Emilia must had decided I wasn't going to be a good provider. I admit I must have showed up on time every day, and I didn't, so that's probably why they fired me: because I was late to work a lot. I must have been crazy to be so lazy on that job at the software company.

   Anyway, here I am—no job, no girl friend. I'm feeling pretty down myself. Let me hear from you, friend.

   R.

8 PERSONALIZATION

This exercise has two parts.

Part 1

You have a problem with your boss in your current job. You are not sure what to do. You like your job and want to do something in order to stay at the job. On a separate piece of paper, write a paragraph telling what you will do and what your boss will do. Use some of the phrases in the box.

> The first thing I could do is . . .
> My boss might . . .
> However, if he listens to me with an open mind, I may . . .
> I have to say something. If I don't, the situation around here will only . . .
> While we're speaking, the discussion could . . .
> I have to be careful of the boss's ego. He has got to be . . .
> I can't lose my temper, or I could . . .
> If I present my case well, I should . . .

Part 2

At your last job, you had a problem getting along with your boss. You believed that he treated you unfairly, so you got angry one day and suddenly quit. Write a paragraph telling what other things you could have done instead of quitting suddenly. Give reasons to explain why these other courses of action could have been better. Use some of the phrases in the box.

> Instead of quitting suddenly, I should have . . .
> When I quit suddenly, my boss must have . . .
> It came as a big surprise to him, so he must not have . . .
> When they heard the news, my colleagues had to have been . . .
> As far as promotions go, I couldn't have . . .
> With a different boss, the atmosphere at work might have . . .
> My boss and I could never have . . .
> In retrospect, I think I shouldn't have . . .

PART III NOUNS

UNIT 6: COUNT AND NON-COUNT NOUNS

1 IDENTIFYING COUNT AND NON-COUNT NOUNS

*In the following passage, write **NC** or **C** to indicate whether the nouns in italics are used as count or non-count in their contexts.*

> Why does *language* (NC) provide such a fascinating object of *study*? Perhaps because of its unique role in capturing the *breadth* of human *thought* and *endeavor*. We look around us and are awed by the variety of several thousand *languages* and *dialects*, expressing a multiplicity of worldviews, *literatures*, and ways of life. We look back at the *thoughts* of our predecessors, and find we can see only as far as *language* lets us see.
>
> We look forward in *time*, and find we can plan only through *language*. We look outward in *space*, and send symbols of *communication* along with our spacecraft, to explain who we are, in case there is anyone out there who wants to know.*

*The passage is taken from David Crystal, *The Cambridge Encyclopedia of Language* (Cambridge: Cambridge University Press, 1987).

2 IDENTIFYING NON-COUNT NOUNS

Read the following article, which discusses the best places for business and careers in the United States. Underline the twenty-six non-count nouns in the article.

At the end of the twentieth century, and after extensive <u>research</u>, we have ranked the nation's biggest metropolitan areas in terms of opportunities for economic growth. We focused on jobs and business, relying on information from U.S. government sources and opinions from expert economists.

Using such criteria as tax friendliness, ease of transportation to and from the region, number of colleges and universities, availability to areas for recreation, and the price of car insurance, we found that Seattle is the best place to be, with its well-known industries of software and aerospace. Many of the winners are also on the west coast, several of them in the Silicon Valley area in California, reputed for its ventures into technology.

A region needs to have overall income development, as well as a high rate of employment and a climate that encourages both investment and enterprise. While high-tech industries currently impart these qualities to many places, other areas are desirable for other reasons. Houston, for example, offers great business opportunities because of its science and medicine, its supply of oil and gas, and because it houses the headquarters of NASA, the National Aeronautics and Space Administration, which directs programs pertaining to space travel and exploration.

Other desirable areas include those around Denver, Atlanta, and Tampa, Florida. What they all have in common is opportunity for economic expansion, and, in the new technological age, an abundance of brainpower.*

*Based on an article in *Forbes Magazine*, May 31, 1999.

Unit 6

3 USING PHRASES TO COUNT NON-COUNT NOUNS

Complete the letter by choosing a phrase from the box. Some phrases will be used more than once, and in some places more than one phrase is appropriate.

a serving of	~~a bit of~~	a slice of
a game of	a glass of	a flash of
a clap of	a period of	a branch of

Dear Mary,

You know how much I dislike picnics. Ted insisted that we go on one before the summer ended, and although I resisted, I am so glad that we finally did that. First, he did all the work. He wouldn't let me do ___a bit of___ work. Of course, he wouldn't
1.
even accept _____ advice from me, either.
2.

We drove off on Saturday morning to Grover's Cove, which is a pleasant, secluded area where we met three other couples. At first the weather was fine. We decided to have _____ volleyball before lunch. But our friends had forgotten the net, so we
3.
forgot about the volleyball game and sat down to play _____ cards and
4.
drink _____ lemonade.
5.

At lunch, as usual, I ate too much. I had _____ Sheila's special
6.
seven-grain bread, _____ Ted's delicious curried chicken salad,
7.
_____ Saga bleu cheese, _____ Sheila's famous
8.   9.
apple pie, and _____ cranberry juice. We settled in to listen to
10.
_____ music by Mozart, the Violin Concerto #3, on the portable CD
11.
player that Robert had brought. Robert's son, by the way, has just gotten his degree in micropaleontology, which is _____ geology. Just as we were dozing off
12.
comfortably on our blankets, we heard _____ thunder, which really startled
13.
us. Then we saw _____ lightning nearby, so we packed up hurriedly
14.

and got into our cars. When we turned on the car radio, we heard _____
                                                                    15.
news: tornadoes were in the area, and it was going to be dangerous to be outside for

_____ *time.*
      16.

We were quite anxious, but we made it home safely and stayed together singing old songs

for the rest of the afternoon. We really had a wonderful day. I'm sorry you weren't with us.

                                                  Love,

                                                  Shelley

4 USING COUNT AND NON-COUNT NOUNS

Read the following article reporting the results of a survey that asked people what they valued most in life. Fill in the blanks in the article, choosing between the forms given.

Survey Results

As expected, _____ good health _____ was cited as the number one factor
                              1. (good health / a good health)

necessary to have a happy life. Having _____ to share
                                                  2. (partner / a partner)

the ups and downs of life was the next most important factor. In describing what

they valued or would value in the partner, people said they wanted to spend their lives

with someone who had _____, who wasn't afraid of
                                     3. (integrity / an integrity)

_____ but at the same time was capable of having
        4. (work / a work)

_____, and who would give _____
   5. (great fun / a great fun)   **6. (love / a love)**

generously. Interestingly, more men than women mentioned that they wanted their

partners to be intelligent. Women tended to mention _____ as
                                                               7. (practicality / a practicality)

a feature they desired in a relationship.

(continued on next page)

Unit 6

The third factor following _____ in
8. (a compatible companion / compatible companion)
importance, was a strong family, cited equally by both sexes. Evidently, people yearn
for connections and _____.
9. (warmth / a warmth)
Also high on the list was having _____ that is
10. (career / a career)
fulfilling, _____ that provides satisfaction.
11. (job / a job)
_____ was not the only consideration; most people said
12. (Good salary / A good salary)
that they also wanted to receive _____ for their work.
13. (respect / a respect)

5 USING COUNT AND NON-COUNT NOUNS

The Ice Cream Association recently published this article in its newsletter. Complete the article by filling in the blanks with the correct form in parentheses.

Ice Cream Association Newsletter

_____Ice cream_____ is rated as Americans' favorite dessert, and it is
1. (An ice cream / Ice cream)
heavily consumed. _____ is estimated to be fifteen quarts
2. (A production / Production)
per year for each person in the United States, and if sherbets and other fruit

concoctions are added, the figure jumps to twenty-three quarts per person.

A kind of ice cream was created in China four thousand years ago. At that

point in _____, people had just begun to get
3. (ancient history / ancient histories)
_____ from farm animals, and the white liquid was a
4. (milk / milks)
prized commodity. _____ of the nobility consisted of a soft
5. (A favorite dish / Favorite dish)
paste made from _____, spices, and milk, and the mixture
6. (overcooked rice / overcooked rices)
was packed in _____ to solidify. This milk ice was
7. (snows / snow)

considered to be _____ of _____
8. (a symbol / symbol)   9. (wealth / a wealth)
at that time. The Chinese also developed various types of desserts made from

_____ combined with different fruits, and by the thirteenth
10. (ices / ice)
century many flavors of these iced desserts were being sold on the streets of Peking.

From China, Marco Polo brought recipes for these wonderful desserts back to fourteenth-century Italy. Before long, frozen desserts traveled from Italy to France. And when Catherine de' Medici married King Henry II of France, she introduced into that country a semifrozen dessert made from _____.
11. (cream / creams)

Soon _____ to quickly freeze the ice cream and iced
12. (a way / way)
fruits developed; by the 1560s these iced products were very popular and sold by street vendors in France and Italy. It is believed that these sweets were introduced to North America by the early English colonists, who made the mixture at home by placing bowls on ice mixed with _____ to create a lower
13. (salt / a salt)
freezing temperature. At the end of the nineteenth century, Italian immigrants added to the popularity of _____ made from fruits; Italian street
14. (the ices / the ice)
vendors, often accompanied by _____, quickly became a
15. (a music / music)
popular sight in cities across North America. Then, in the 1920s, an Ohio man introduced the first chocolate-covered vanilla ice cream bar on

_____, calling it a "Good Humor Sucker." From this
16. (stick / a stick)
concept of good humor evolved the well-known Good Humor man, who to this day continues to drive his small musical truck up and down the streets of American towns, bringing _____ to children everywhere.*
17. (happiness / a happiness)

*Based on Charles Panati, *Extraordinary Origins of Everyday Things* (Perennial Library, Harper & Row, 1987, revised 1989).

6 EDITING

Read the following article. Find and correct the fourteen errors in the use of count and non-count nouns.

Spoken language is a wonderful thing, enabling us to communicate feelings and thoughts, to tell stories and even lies. Early in history of mankind, use of symbols to communicate ideas went one step further. It was not necessary to be in actual proximity to another human being when one could send signals by smokes or drums. But, how could this communications be kept in any permanent form?

People began to record markings on hard surfaces like a clay, using symbols to represent peoples, animals, or, later, various abstraction. Over many thousands of years, the pictures developed into different alphabet.

What would the world be like without writing and reading? How would knowledges pass from one generation to another? Yet writing and reading were not always skill to be taken for granted. In fact, until recent generations, a literacy has not been as common as it is now.

What about the future? Technology is advancing the ways we have of disseminating informations. One hundred years from now, computer literacies will be as commonplace and necessary as reading and writing are now.

7 PERSONALIZATION

People differ greatly in their likes and dislikes. How would you describe yours? Write about yourself. Include some of the phrases from this box.

> Some of my favorite foods are . . .
> My favorite cuisine is . . .
> My favorite beverages are . . .
> My least favorite food is . . .
> Some of the activities I like most are . . .
> Activities I dislike include . . .
> In school, my favorite subjects were . . .
> In school, my least favorite subjects were . . .
> Two sports that I like are . . .
> Two careers that interest me are . . .
> For me, the most important things in life are . . .

UNIT 7
DEFINITE AND INDEFINITE ARTICLES

1 USING ARTICLES

Read the following ads for job seekers that appear on an environmental jobs page on the Internet. Select the correct article in each set of parentheses (write **0** if no article is needed).

Associate Zoological Veterinarian

Requires a degree in ____0____ veterinary medicine from
          1. (a / 0)
_____ recognized university, and two to three years of
2. (a / the)
_____ experience in _____ medical care
3. (an / 0)   4. (a / the)
of wild animals in a zoological institute. Extensive knowledge of
_____ wildlife and _____ wildlife behavior
5. (the / 0)   6. (a / 0)
is highly desirable. _____ salary is above average.
                      7. (The / A)
Excellent benefits.

Coordinator of Endangered Species

This is _____ unique opportunity for _____ experienced and
      8. (0 / a)   9. (an / 0)
highly motivated professional to deal with issues regarding endangered species. Three years in _____ program or institute protecting endangered species is
           10. (a / the)
necessary, and one year at a technical or professional level in _____
                                                              11. (the / 0)
researching and analyzing data. A Master's degree or higher is desirable. Salary: $3,866 per month, plus generous benefits.

Fisheries Biologist

Our small commercial company needs _____ field biologist to test fish on
                                    12. (a / the)
commercial fishing boats off _____ coast of Alaska. _____
                              13. (0 / the)   14. (A / The)
position requires a Master's degree in _____ biology or other natural
                                        15. (the / 0)
science, _____ college-level statistics course, and _____ flexible
         16. (the / a)   17. (a / the)
attitude. Applicants can expect strenuous working conditions, but _____
                                                                  18. (a / the)
good salary commensurate with their experience. Apply to _____ head
                                                          19. (a / the)
office in Juneau.

Environmental Microbiology

_____ Department of _____ Civil Engineering at _____
20. (A / The)   21. (the / 0)   22. (the / 0)
University of Atlantis invites _____ applications for _____
                                23. (an / 0)   24. (an / the)
associate professor position. We are particularly interested in candidates with

_____ extensive experience in _____ research.
25. (an / 0)   26. (the / 0)
The successful candidate will demonstrate a background of high-quality teaching at the undergraduate and graduate levels, and must have a Ph.D. _____
                                                                                27. (The / A)
highest salary is offered.

2 USING ARTICLES

Read the following passage on the development of language and choose the correct article to fill the blanks (write 0 if no article is needed).

Scholars do not agree on ____the____ degree of sophistication of language of the
1. (the / a)

early human beings; however, we can imagine how language might have developed

among them. One theory of _____ beginnings of language is described here briefly.
2. (the / 0)

As _____ animals have the ability and need to communicate, so do
3. (the / 0)

_____ human beings. Primitive people, like people today, could make contact
4. (the / 0)

with _____ outside world by means of their five senses. They could see
5. (the / an)

_____ other human beings, animals, and inanimate objects; they could hear
6. (an / 0)

their sounds and the sounds of _____ environment. Also like animals, these
7. (the / 0)

early people did not live alone. They lived in _____ groups. By doing so, they
8. (the / 0)

avoided _____ loneliness, helped each other in the hunting and gathering of
9. (the / 0)

_____ food, and protected themselves from _____ danger. Group life
10. (the / 0)   11. (a / 0)

made communication all the more important.

Various ways to communicate developed. Primitive people used _____
12. (a / 0)

sound, gestures, and touch. _____ grunting sound might have indicated that
13. (A / 0)

_____ rock was too heavy to lift alone, or _____ gesture might have
14. (the / a)   15. (a / 0)

meant "Come here" or "I'm hungry." _____ touch could have expressed
16. (A / 0)

_____ tenderness or love. Over time, _____ words evolved from
17. (the / 0)   18. (the / 0)

sounds that represented objects and actions important to primitive people's lives.*

---

*Based on "Communication Mediums: Primitive Means," *Compton's Encyclopedia, Online Edition,* downloaded from *America Online,* November 18, 1994.

3 USING ARTICLES

*In the following letter, fill in the blanks with the correct form in parentheses (write **0** if no article is needed).*

Dear Ricardo,

Things have gotten better since I last wrote to you. First, I received ___a___ letter
                                                                    1. (a / 0)
from my family with _____ very nice surprise in it: _____ check for
                    2. (the / a)   3. (the / a)
$200. _____ letter made me feel good because I thought my family had forgotten
      4. (A / The)
me, and _____ check made me feel even better. With _____ money,
        5. (the / 0)   6. (the / a)
I went to _____ expensive restaurant downtown with _____ new
          7. (an / 0)   8. (the / a)
friend. Yes, _____ new friend is _____ beautiful young woman. If our
             9. (the / a)   10. (the / a)
relationship develops, I'll tell you her name in _____ next letter I write to you.
                                                 11. (the / 0)
What I will tell you now is that she is _____ only daughter of _____
                                        12. (the / an)   13. (the / 0)
president of my university.

_____ weather has improved, too. We haven't had _____ rain for
14. (The / A)   15. (the / 0)
three weeks now; I've seen _____ sun every day, and last weekend I went to
                           16. (the / a)
_____ beach and got _____ suntan.
17. (a / 0)   18. (the / a)

Do you know anything about _____ American football? It's _____
                           19. (the / 0)   20. (a / the)
really rough game played by two teams with eleven people on each team. _____
                                                                        21. (The / A)
team that has _____ ball is suppose to take it into the opposing team's territory
              22. (the / 0)
and score _____ touchdown—that means they get six points. At first, I didn't
          23. (the / a)
understand it, but I've gone to a few games and I see that it's exciting but more dangerous
than _____ game we play at home that we call football. Here they call our game
     24. (a / the)
_____ soccer.
25. (the / 0)

My classes are going better, too. I like _____ organic chemistry and
                                          26. (the / 0)
_____ computer science. I even like _____ history now; this course
27. (the / 0)   28. (the / 0)

(continued on next page)

focuses on _____ most important events of the twentieth century. I still don't like
          29. (the / 0)
_____ English, though. I am just not very good in _____ languages.
  30. (the / 0)   31. (the / 0)
Well, Ricardo, I gotta go! That's _____ American English way of saying
                                     32. (0 / the)
"I have got to go." Write me soon, OK?

                                                                Marco

4 USING ARTICLES

Complete the archaeologist's report about planet Green by supplying the articles **a**, **an**, and **the** where appropriate. Use **0** to indicate no article.

SITE: _____
DATE: _____
NOTES: _____

Remains were found of what appears to be ____a____ large city on
                                              1.
_____ island in _____ Northern Hemisphere. It seems that
     2.   3.
_____ city was part of _____ advanced civilization.
     4.   5.
What we had thought was _____ sophisticated canal system has
                              6.
turned out to be something else entirely. _____ canals that we thought we
                                                 7.
saw contained no water but were covered with _____ hard surface. We
                                                    8.
think these were actually _____ roadways that _____ vehicles
                                 9.   10.
traveled on. _____ vehicles had four wheels, and _____ pieces
                    11.   12.
from _____ thousands of them were seen. _____ shadows that
            13.   14.
we had seen by telescope were actually _____ buildings, very tall buildings,
                                                15.
that _____ population probably lived in. We found no agricultural areas,
          16.
although we did find _____ large grassy space in _____ middle
                            17.   18.
of _____ island. We are not sure how the inhabitants obtained their food;
      19.

probably they brought it by boat from _____20._____ *mainland, or over* _____21._____ *bridge. We also found* _____22._____ *parallel rows of* _____23._____ *iron, perhaps used for some form of* _____24._____ *transportation. We suspect that the inhabitants traveled by air, too, but we didn't find* _____25._____ *evidence of any type of airport or air transportation vehicles. We are not sure why* _____26._____ *area was abandoned, but maybe it was because* _____27._____ *entire planet was suffering from* _____28._____ *severe pollution.*

5 USING THE DEFINITE ARTICLE OR 0 ARTICLE WITH NAMES

A travel agent has sent this letter to her client, along with plane and hotel tickets. Complete the letter by filling in the blanks with **the** *where the definite article is needed and with* **0** *where the definite article is not needed.*

GLOBE TRAVEL

Dear Dorothea:

You will leave _____0_____ Los Angeles at 11 P.M. You'll be flying at night, so you
                    1.
won't see _____ Rocky Mountains or _____ Mississippi River,
              2.   3.
which is really a pity.

After you leave _____ United States, you'll be flying off the coast of
                       4.
_____ Canada, then over _____ Atlantic to _____
     5.   6.   7.
United Kingdom. As you fly over _____ Europe, you will be able to see
                                          8.
_____ France as you cross _____ Alps into _____
     9.   10.   11.
Switzerland. You'll land in _____ Geneva.
                                     12.

You have reservations at _____ Sheraton Hotel where the conference is.
                                    13.

(continued on next page)

I've reserved a place for you on the post-conference tour to _____ Hungary
14.
and _____ Czech Republic, so you'll be able to see a little of eastern
15.
Europe. You'll be coming home on a different route, as you requested, so that you can
stop in _____ Florida to see your grandmother. It's too bad you won't be
16.
able to visit _____ Bahamas or _____ Dominican Republic while
17. 18.
you're in the area, as _____ Caribbean is a great place to relax after the
19.
hard work you will have been doing at the conference.

Your return flight is at 8 A.M. on Monday, the fifteenth, and you arrive home at 10:20 A.M.

Have a great trip!

6 USING ARTICLES

Read Radio Station KESL's interview with popular disc jockey Nancy Stone. Complete the interview by filling in the blanks with the correct article (write 0 if no article # is needed).

KESL: So, Nancy, why do you think _____0_____ rock music is still so popular?
1. (a / 0)

STONE: Well, _____ rock music that I play on this station is classic and speaks to
2. (the / 0)
_____ people everywhere. There are many variations of _____
3. (a / 0) 4. (the / 0)
rock, and I choose music that I know people will respond to, _____ best
5. (the / 0)
songs, those that speak to _____ heart.
6. (the / 0)

KESL: Do you mean songs about _____ love?
7. (the / 0)

STONE: Yes, of course, but also songs about _____ pain and _____
8. (a / 0) 9. (a / 0)
longing.

KESL: Who are _____ most popular artists?
10. (the / a)

STONE: My show plays mostly _____ classic rock, you know, so we play a lot of
11. (a / 0)
the golden oldies, like the Beatles, the Rolling Stones, even Elvis. Elton John

Definite and Indefinite Articles

remains _____ popular artist, maybe because of his association with
12. (a / the)
_____ Princess Diana.
13. (the / 0)

KESL: What about _____ country music?
14. (a / 0)

STONE: I, personally, like _____ country music that I hear these days.
15. (a / the)
_____ line between country and rock is not as clear as it used to be.
16. (The / A)
Until recently, the themes of country music—_____ abandonment,
17. (the / 0)
_____ prison, _____ driving in trucks—were not what our
18. (the / 0)   19. (a / 0)
listeners liked to hear. Now, though, singers like Garth Brooks and Winona are
superstars, and _____ songs they sing appeal to almost everybody.
20. (the / 0)

KESL: Any international songs?

STONE: Yes. We play some songs of Ricky Martin, or whoever is hot at the time, and sometimes we have requests for old favorites of groups like Los Lobos. Their music is well known, and it's not necessary to speak _____ language
21. (the / a)
in order to appreciate them.

KESL: So _____ same music is appreciated all over _____ world?
22. (the / a)   23. (the / 0)

STONE: It seems so. I've heard _I Want to Hold Your Hand_ in elevators from _____
24. (the / 0)
United States to _____ Europe to _____ Far East; I've heard
25. (the / 0)   26. (the / 0)
La Macarena on the stereo while flying over _____ Andes Mountains and
27. (the / 0)
over _____ Atlantic on _____ Concorde, even while flying over
28. (the / 0)   29. (the / a)
_____ North Pole. Whether I stay in _____ Hilton Hotel in
30. (the / 0)   31. (the / 0)
Chicago or _____ Hilton Hotel in Cairo, _____ music is
32. (the / 0)   33. (the / 0)
_____ same. Culturally, you know, _____ planet is getting
34. (the / 0)   35. (the / a)
smaller and smaller.

KESL: What about Peter, Paul, and Mary, or folk singers like Joan Baez?

STONE: Never. Well, almost never. _____ only time I play Peter, Paul, and Mary is
36. (The / 0)
at _____ Christmas. They recorded _____ Christmas concert at
37. (the / 0)   38. (a / 0)
_____ end of _____ 1980s that people like to hear during
39. (the / an)   40. (the / 0)
_____ holiday season.
41. (the / a)

(continued on next page)

Unit 7

KESL: Do you play any groups from Woodstock?

STONE: You mean the original Woodstock, _____ one from '69? Occasionally I
            42. (0 / the)
have _____ request for the Grateful Dead, or maybe for Janis Joplin. But I
     43. (the / a)
don't play anything from Woodstock '99.

KESL: By the way, I've heard that some of _____ presidents have been
                                                44. (the / 0)
enthusiastic fans of pop music.

STONE: Right. I remember that _____ President Bush was _____
                                  45. (the / 0)   46. (the / a)
country music fan, and President Clinton used to like _____ song called
                                                       47. (a / 0)
Chelsea Morning; in fact, he named his daughter Chelsea because he liked

_____ song so much.
48. (the / a)

KESL: What's your all-time favorite, Nancy?

STONE: Oh, I don't know Bob. Actually, I'll tell you _____ secret: I really like
                                                          49. (a / 0)
_____ classical music most of all.
50. (the / 0)

7 EDITING

Read the following bulletin. Find and correct the twenty-one errors in the use of articles, either by supplying the correct article or by omitting the article.

METROPOLITAN ZOO

Your Metropolitan Zoo needs you! Can you adopt *an* animal? You can "adopt" an animal by contributing money for its care. By adopting an animal, you will help us keep zoo in good condition with the healthy animals, and you will have a satisfaction of knowing that your love and your efforts are keeping "your" animal alive and well. Which animal would you like to adopt?

Needing adoption right now are: two tigers, one lion, two camels, a family of three chimpanzees, and one gorilla.

Here is some information about the animals needing adoption. Both our tigers are female; we are hoping to obtain male from Pakistan next year. A lion, recently named Mufasa by a group of the schoolchildren, is three years old. Both camels are Arabian kind, with one hump, not Bactrian kind, with two humps. Chimpanzees in our zoo act just like human family. They take care of each other, laugh, and sometimes even have the arguments. We have only one gorilla now; he is most popular animal at zoo, and also most expensive to maintain. He needs several sponsors. He puts on the show every afternoon by interacting with a visitors. He loves an applause that he gets.

After you adopt, you will regularly be advised of a life situation of your animal. You will be honored at our annual spring banquet, and you will receive free admission to a zoo.

Please find it in your heart to contribute to well-being of our animals.

8 PERSONALIZATION

Write a letter describing your hometown to someone who is about to visit there for the first time. Describe the character of your hometown and the most important places to see. Include some of the phrases in the box.

> When you come to my hometown, you will first notice the atmosphere of . . .
>
> The most prominent physical feature of my hometown is . . .
>
> The most prominent building in my hometown is . . .
>
> Some interesting things to see in my hometown include . . .
>
> Be sure to visit . . .
>
> In the evening, you can go to . . .
>
> The people are friendly and show a lot of . . .
>
> Near the center of town, you will find . . .
>
> My hometown is noted for . . .
>
> Although my hometown is new and modern, it doesn't have . . .
>
> Fortunately / Unfortunately, my hometown has / doesn't have . . .
>
> I'm sure you will like . . .
>
> What I miss about my hometown is . . .

UNIT 8

MODIFICATION OF NOUNS

1 PUTTING MODIFIERS IN APPROPRIATE ORDER

Complete the following review of a fashion show by filling in the blanks with the modifiers placed in their correct order. Place commas where necessary.

Last week at _____the annual fashion_____ show in Paris,
         1. (fashion / the / annual)
_____ designers displayed their latest
    2. (young / some / bright)
creations. Everybody had expected _____
                                     3. (these / spring / new)
fashions to be similar to last year's rather ordinary and boring
clothes; instead, the designers delighted the audience with a brilliant
presentation. Drawing on _____ inspirations,
                          4. (different / many / international)
they showed _____ collection in a decade.
              5. (first / exciting / the / new)
Maurice Isak's inspiration came from the Orient;
_____ lines without _____
 6. (his / clean / long)   7. (extra / much)
ornamentation, done in _____ fabrics,
                         8. (expensive / fine / silk)
obviously recalled _____ paintings. He
                     9. (Japanese / old / some)
translated _____ ideas into
            10. (classic / simple / these)
_____ suits and gave them
   11. (elegant / business)
_____ touch. Another designer,
   12. (soft / a / feminine)
Louis Darrieux, had apparently visited Tahiti, as evidenced by
_____ outfits, which bring to mind images of
 13. (brightly colored / his / wild)
_____ islands and which are perfect for
 14. (far-off / tropical / South Sea)

(continued on next page)

Unit 8

_____ wear. But inspiration for _____
15. (casual / daytime)   16. (liveliest / new / the)
clothes came from Mexico, in Guillermo Pérez's collection. _____
                                                                  17. (pink / hot / those)
hues combined with _____ colors woven together with
                        18. (purple / brilliant / several)
turquoise and orange in _____ skirts were the sensation
                            19. (cotton / long / flowing)
of the show.

It has been a long time since we have seen such beautiful styles from

_____ designer; we are pleased as punch to have
20. (well-known / any / contemporary)

_____ artists among us.
21. (new / fabulous / these)

❷ USING NOUN MODIFIERS

Complete the following passage by turning the phrases listed in the box into noun modifier constructions. Then write them in the appropriate blanks.

cats that live in the house	jam made of strawberries
dogs that belong to a family	a table in the kitchen
dreams of childhood	tea made of blackberries
horses used for work	a sister who is a baby
memories of childhood	a house for dogs
horses displayed in shows	a night in the summer
gardens where flowers grow	~~trees that grow apples~~
a pie made of peaches	gardens where vegetables grow

My happiest memories are of visiting my grandparents' farm every summer when I was a child. There they had many _____apple trees_____ that I used to climb to pick
                                                    1.
the apples. They had both _____, where roses and violets grew,
                                    2.
and _____, from which we gathered the carrots and beans that
        3.
we ate at dinner.

There were some horses—_____—which helped my
                                    4.
grandfather and the men in the fields, and even a few _____,
                                                              5.

which won prizes in the state fairs. There were a lot of cats, but they weren't _____ 6. _____; they roamed outside, particularly in the barn area, hunting the mice. There were always the beloved _____ 7. _____, too, that patrolled the fields and protected us from intruders. Usually they slept outside in the special _____ 8. _____ that Grandfather had made, but Pluto, my favorite, was allowed to sleep on my bed.

When we were alone, my grandmother used to make her own jellies and jams; I loved to pick the strawberries in the fields to make my contribution to her special _____ 9. _____. She also made a delicious tea from the wild blackberries growing nearby. I would have that wonderful _____ 10. _____ at night, along with a piece of _____ 11. _____ that she made from her own home-grown peaches. We would sit at the _____ 12. _____ after clearing off the dinner dishes and talk about life, about her _____ 13. _____ of so many years earlier and about my _____ 14. _____ for the future.

Then she would gently lead me to the small, cozy bedroom that I shared with my _____ 15. _____, who was too young then to appreciate the beautiful times with my grandmother. I slept soundly and peacefully every _____ 16. _____ that I spent at my grandmother's house and dreamed almost every night in the intervening winters that I was basking in the warmth of her love.

3 FORMING COMPOUND MODIFIERS

Following is a list of items recently purchased at Joseph and Lillian's Antique Shop. Rewrite each item as a noun with modifiers including a compound modifier.

Joseph and Lillian's Antique Shop

1. 2 silver candlesticks — ninety-five years old
   Two ninety-five-year-old silver candlesticks

2. 1 dining room table — 200 years old

3. 8 dining room chairs — covered in velvet

4. 2 Tiffany lamps — century old

5. 1 samovar — plated in silver

6. 1 chandelier — leaded with crystal

7. 2 rocking chairs — 150 years old

8. 1 Persian carpet — woven by hand

9. 1 manuscript — written by hand

10. 3 coffee tables — inlaid with ivory

11. 4 serving dishes — painted by hand

12. 2 mahogany beds — carved by hand

13. 2 vases — 130 years old / inlaid with gold

4 USING NOUN MODIFIERS

The following personal statement was part of an application sent to a graduate business school. Supply the missing modifiers in the letter from the box below.

activities for students who are international	an award from five states for volunteerism
award given for four years of service	~~camp where boys go in the summer~~
council for ethics of students	disorder that is a deficit in paying attention
houses that are old and dilapidated	store for convenience that is local

I hope to enrich my life by attending the John K. Smith School of Business. There, I will grow and refine my abilities by enhancing the knowledge I already have about business. I am bringing a lot of leadership experience to the school, and sincere eagerness to learn. During the past five years, I have been active in community and university activities, and I have won several awards. I have been:

1. a tennis coach at a ____boys'____ ____summer____ ____camp____

2. the weekend manager at a _____ _____ _____

3. the president of the _____ _____ _____ for ethical behavior at my university

4. the coordinator of the _____ _____ _____ for foreign students at my university

5. a volunteer who fixes up _____ _____ _____ for better community housing commission

6. a volunteer who works in the public school system with children who have _____ _____ _____

7. the recipient of the _____-_____ _____ _____, in appreciation for service during four years of undergraduate school

8. the recipient of the _____-_____ _____ _____, for the most valuable contributions to volunteerism in five states

(continued on next page)

I hope I can further enrich my career and my life by attending your school. If I am fortunate enough to do so, I expect to make the John K. Smith School of Management proud of me as a graduate.

I am looking forward to hearing from you soon.

Very truly yours,

Edward T. Larson

Edward T. Larson

5 EDITING

Read the following passage about a writer's first days in New York. Find and correct the sixteen errors in the modification of nouns.

                fresh country
Moving from the ~~country fresh~~ air to the head-clogging, polluted stuff they still call air presents a shock to the body. Having miraculously obtained a paying job in the, to me, publishing glamorous world, I moved with my wife and two daughters from southwest beautiful Montana with its blue, clear skies to New York, where there appeared to us to be no skies at all, only gray, dirty smog.

    Within a week, my wife and children came down with a respiratory mysterious ailment. Coughing and sneezing, with eyes and nose dripping, they suffered noisily for ten days. A ten-days siege in a cramped four-rooms apartment felt like being imprisoned in a dreary, jail, cement cell. Just as the three of them were recovering from the insult to the body and soul, I succumbed to it. After only two weeks at my new prized job, I had to call in sick. And was I sick! My forty-two-years-old, feverish body ached as it never had before. Iron gigantic hammers pounded in my head. My lungs felt like black lead, huge weights. I coughed constantly, so that I never had more than a two-hours rest, even though I took double the recommended dose of the over-the-counter cough medication we had bought at a corner drug store. Finally, after ten days, I too, recovered physically, although not psychologically, from my New York unspeakably rude reception. My three first weeks in the Big Apple gave me the feeling that I lived in a foreign and hostile country—and I still live there.

6 PERSONALIZATION

What do you hope for in the future for your family and for yourself? What do you expect that you and they will be doing in five years? In ten years? When you or they are sixty-five years old? Select one person or some people from each group (1–3) below and write a few sentences about each of your selections. Use as many of the types of modifiers from the box as you can.

1. My mother / my sister / my wife / my daughter / my best female friend
2. My father / my brother / my husband / my son / my best male friend
3. My parents / my brothers and sisters / my children / my best friends

TYPES OF MODIFIERS	
Determiners	a, an, the, this, those, his, her
Quantifiers	one, two, few, little, many, some
Adjectives	of opinion (nice); qualities (heavy); size (big); age (old)
Nouns	apple tree, shoe store, six-lane highway

Example:

In five years, I expect that I will be living with my wife in a nice upscale two-bedroom apartment in this town. We may have one baby by that time, and we'll be planning to move into a larger place—maybe an old country house. In about ten years, we'll be at the peak of our careers and will probably have two healthy, beautiful children. Since we expect to make a lot of money, we'll be able to retire long before age sixty-five, and we'll be experienced world travelers.

_____
_____
_____
_____
_____
_____
_____

UNIT 9

QUANTIFIERS

1 IDENTIFYING QUANTIFIERS

The following message is from the International Almanac for a year early in the twenty-first century. Underline the twenty-five quantifiers.

The International Almanac

From November through March, a lot of warmer-than-usual weather is expected in the Northern Hemisphere, although not in every area. Certain parts of Europe—especially the British Isles and France—will be warm, but some parts of North America—notably western Canada and Alaska—will be somewhat colder. In western Africa, the weather will be cooler than usual, and with less rain; this is good news for people in the Caribbean and the eastern seaboard of the United States, as these conditions will probably lead to fewer hurricanes than usual in those areas. However, in Africa itself, the condition of too little precipitation will continue, and there probably won't be enough rain to produce all the crops necessary to feed the population. Elsewhere in the Southern Hemisphere, a beautiful spring and summer are predicted in South America. No tidal waves are expected this year in Australia or Japan, nor are other weather problems expected in either place.

From April through October, we will have more warm weather in a few parts of Europe, but on most of the Continent, temperatures will remain close to normal. There won't be much snow in the Alps before the end of October; after that, plenty of snow is expected and should ensure a successful ski season. The amount of snow in the Andes will be normal, as will the temperatures throughout the rest of South America. In North America, the waters of the Mississippi will be high, due to a great deal of rain; we can expect two floods, neither of which will be as serious as the floods of the summer of 1993. A number of earthquakes are expected to occur during this period in Asia, but none of them will be major.

The levels of both the Atlantic and the Pacific oceans will remain the same, even though over the long term each of them is expected to rise. The hole in the ozone layer over Antarctica is expected to become slightly larger, thus permitting more harmful ultraviolet rays to enter the atmosphere. By this time next year, however, the news about the ozone layer may be better because of the efforts, many of which are proving successful, to control the greenhouse effect.

2 USING QUANTIFIERS

Complete the following letter by selecting the correct quantifiers.

Dear Marco,

Well, you certainly seem to be having __a lot of__ fun in the
                                      1. (a lot of / many)
United States now. I see that _____ friends in your life
                                  2. (a few / a little)
makes _____ difference to your state of mind. You should
        3. (a number of / a great deal of)
send _____ news about the lady you wrote about. Is she
      4. (a little / a few)
special, or do you have _____ girlfriends? You never used to
                          5. (many / much)
have _____ girlfriends at all, Marco. What happened? Did you
      6. (any / no)
have _____ luck suddenly? Did you suddenly get handsome?
      7. (a couple of / a bit of)

(continued on next page)

Are _____ 8. (a great deal of / all) the girls calling you up every day? If I sound jealous, I am. _____ 9. (A little / A couple of) weeks ago you were complaining that _____ 10. (either / every) person you had met was ignoring you; now it seems that you have _____ 11. (an amount of / a bunch of) friends and that you are even doing well in _____ 12. (a couple of / a bit of) your classes. I, on the other hand, may fail _____ 13. (a great deal of / most of) my classes. Besides that, I lost _____ 14. (a great many / a lot of) money last month when I invested in a "get-rich-quick" scheme. I borrowed money from everybody, and now I owe _____ 15. (many / a great deal of) money to _____ 16. (a bit of / a few of) our friends. Marco, do you think that you could lend me _____ 17. (a few / a little) money? I'll pay you back soon.

Your friend,

Ricardo

3 USING QUANTIFIERS

Complete the selection by choosing quantifiers.

There are ____fewer____ 1. (few / fewer / less) monkeys and apes living now than previously, as their habitats are being destroyed by various human activities. There is _____ 2. (fewer / less / few) habitable land than there used to be because of extensive development by humans.

_____ 3. (Many / Much / A lot) species of monkeys are in imminent danger of becoming extinct because of _____ 4. (any / many / a great deal of) habitat loss. _____ 5. (Many / Much / A great deal of) areas in the rain forests of South America, Asia, and Africa have been totally destroyed, jeopardizing the survival of _____ 6. (some / some of / any) species. International laws now place _____ 7. (many / much / every) animals on lists of endangered species. While such laws protect individual animals to some extent, they have not prevented habitat destruction.

Because of protective laws, _____ 8. (some / few / a few) species of monkeys or apes

are used for commercial purposes any longer. There is one kind of monkey, however, the rhesus monkey, that has been used in _____ medical and
9. (a lot of / many / a great many)
psychological research during recent decades. Although _____
10. (some / any / a little)
rhesus monkeys remain in their natural habitat, _____
11. (a great amount of / a great deal of / a great number of)
these monkeys are also raised in captivity now for research needs.

4 USING QUANTIFIERS

Read the passage from the business section of a newspaper about choosing a financial advisor. Fill in the blanks with one of the items from the box above each part.

More and more people are using the Internet to make their financial transactions on their own. Although in some cases this practice is economical and profitable, in many cases it appears that the advice of an experienced financial planner would be in order.

| expertise | ~~financial planner~~ | paycheck | professional advice | time |

Who needs a __financial planner__ to help plan finances? People whose income and
1.
assets are more than just a _____ need one. If you don't have any
2.
_____ because you're too busy, or if, although highly intelligent, you
3.
have no _____ in the area of money, you may benefit from some
4.
_____.
5.

| goals | professionals | retirement | vacation | year |

You want to improve your current financial situation but don't know where to start, or you want to plan for inevitable expenses such as buying a home, caring for an aging parent, or financing a child's education. What about _____ while you're
6.
young enough to enjoy it? How about being able to take a _____ or
7.
two every _____? For these and many other _____,
8. 9.
you could benefit from the advice of one of a number of _____.
10.

(continued on next page)

Unit 9

| expert | insurance | interests | money | specialty | stock market | trust |

What kind of professional? Financial advisors may have a _____ in
___11.___
_____. Or he or she may be an _____ in the
___12.___   ___13.___
_____. Whatever the specialty, the advisor must have your
___14.___
_____ at heart. You shouldn't invest too much _____
___15.___   ___16.___
with the advisor at first. After you feel that the advisor is looking out for your financial

welfare, you will probably develop a great deal of _____ in him or her.
                                                    ___17.___

But, remember that you are the boss. The financial planner may guide you in the right

direction, but you are the one who sets the direction.

5 USING QUANTIFIERS

Read the information and complete it by choosing the appropriate quantifiers.

Almost _____*every*_____ adult in the United States has been invited to
       1. (every / either / all)
use a credit card at _____ time. Usually an "invitation" to use
                     2. (some / any / each)
one comes in the mail, along with a _____ of flattering remarks
                                    3. (great amount / number / great deal)
about the exclusivity of the people chosen to use the card.

The temptation to take out the credit card is strong, especially among

_____ people who are not highly creditworthy at the time they
4. (certain / a certain / every)
receive the offer, such as students or recent graduates. The prospect of having

_____ desirable goods so easily attainable with a little plastic
5. (much of / much / many)
card can be extremely seductive.

_____ cards are issued by individual stores and are good only
6. (An amount of / Much / Some)
for purchases within the store. Others are issued by banks, through MasterCard or VISA,

for example, and still others by the credit card companies themselves, such as American Express and Diners Club. _____ oil companies and telephone
7. (Either of the / Any of the / Some)
companies, too, issue cards to large numbers of users.

_____ the credit cards work the same way. The consumer
8. (Most of / Much of / A great deal of)
makes purchases and receives bills in the mail within a month. What he or she doesn't pay that month is subject to interest, often at a rate as high as 18 percent. Large stores and services usually have systems set up to bill the customer directly. The bank cards work somewhat differently. When a customer uses the card to purchase an item, the credit card issuer pays the store but deducts _____ money from this
9. (an amount of / a number of / a few)
payment as a service charge. The credit card issuer therefore profits from service charges and from interest charges and, in most cases, also profits from an annual fee charged to the consumer for the privilege of using the card.

_____ way, paying the store directly or paying the credit card
10. (Neither / Both / Either)
company, if the customer doesn't pay within _____ time, he or
11. (a certain / certain / little)
she must pay interest. Of course, the more he or she pays at once, the _____ interest the customer will have to pay in total.
12. (fewer / little / less)

6 EDITING

Read the following first draft of a letter from an investment counseling service. Find and correct the thirteen errors in the use of quantifiers. (In each case, change the quantifier; do not change other words.)

Smith & Fitch

Dear Investor:

    We know that you are a financially responsible citizen who doesn't have ~~no~~ *any* time to study the financial markets or enough expertise to carry out sophisticated financial dealings. A few people these days can keep up with financial developments. Because

(continued on next page)

people can't keep up, we at Smith & Fitch Investing Service are here to provide investment counseling for you.

Right now you are probably overwhelmed by having to think about the short-term and long-term needs of your family, that is, either their immediate needs and their future needs. Let us offer you a financial plan to keep you on top of your expenses and in control of your life so that you will have fewer anxiety and many more money.

We will create a portfolio for you that includes every of your assets. We will provide you with the number of information you need to make your financial decisions and several advice that comes from almost eight decades of experience. We are fully aware of each of the news that will impact your investments, and we can act promptly not only to preserve your capital, but also to put it to the most advantageous use.

Of course, you should be diversified in your investments. We will make sure your portfolio has the right mix of stocks and bonds. You can even work with a few stock options that will earn you a few extra money. At your age, you could do very well with an annuity or a life insurance policy; neither of those will preserve your capital very safely. There are a great deal of possible scenarios; we want to develop the one that is best for you personally. We will give your situation a great number of thought and will always be available for consultation.

Please call us soon to set up an appointment.

Very truly yours,

Fred Fitch

Smith & Fitch

7 PERSONALIZATION

If you win the lottery, what will you do with the money? Write some of your ideas. Include some of the phrases from the box.

> First, I will pay all . . .
> Then I will put a little . . .
> I will invest in some . . .
> I will take a few . . .
> I will buy many . . .
> I might buy a couple of . . .
> I will contribute to certain . . .
> I will finally have enough . . .
> I will give some . . .
> I will relax and have a lot of . . .

PART IV ADJECTIVE CLAUSES AND PHRASES

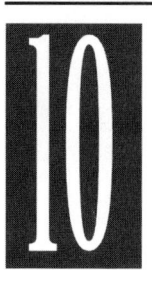

UNIT 10
ADJECTIVE CLAUSES: REVIEW AND EXPANSION

1 IDENTIFYING ADJECTIVE CLAUSES

Read the following article about an invention and its inventor. Underline the twenty-three adjective clauses. (Remember that some adjective clauses do not have a relative pronoun.)

LIQUID PAPER

This is the story of a very simple invention <u>that you can find in almost every office in the whole world today</u>. It is also the story of an inventor whose creativity and persistence resulted in a very useful product. What is the famous invention? It is Liquid Paper, the white liquid that covers up the mistakes you make when writing or typing. It was invented by Bette Nesmith Graham, a secretary in Dallas, Texas, in the early 1950s, who began using tempera paint to cover up the typing errors in her work.

At the time, she was a twenty-seven-year-old single mother of one son, struggling to make ends meet and working as a secretary to the chairman of a big Dallas bank. When she began to work with her first electric typewriter, she found that the type marks she typed onto the paper didn't erase as cleanly as those from manual typewriters. So Ms. Nesmith, who was also an artist, quietly began painting out her mistakes. Soon she was supplying bottles of her homemade preparation, which she called Mistake Out, to other secretaries in the building.

When she lost her job with the company, she turned to working full time to develop the Mistake Out as a business, expanding from her house into a small trailer she had bought for the backyard. In hopes of marketing her product, she approached IBM, which turned her down. She stepped up her own marketing and within a decade was a financial success. The product, which came to be called Liquid Paper, was manufactured in four countries and sold in nearly three dozen. In fiscal 1979, which ended about six months before she sold the company, it had sales of $38 million, of which $3.5 million was net income. By the time she finally sold her business to Gillette in 1979, she had built her simple, practical idea into a $47.5 million business.

It is heartwarming that the story has a happy ending in more ways than one. Ms. Nesmith remarried and became Mrs. Graham. Her son, Michael, a musician of whom she is understandably proud, became very successful as one of a music group called the Monkees, which appeared on an NBC television show for several years in the mid-1960s. Subsequently a country-rock musician, a songwriter, and a video producer, he now heads a production company in California, where he also directs some charities.

With some of her profits, Mrs. Graham established a foundation whose purpose is to provide leading intellectuals with the time, space, and compatible colleagues that they need to ponder and articulate the most important social problems of our era. Bette Nesmith Graham first developed a product that there was clearly a need for; then she used the substantial profits for charitable purposes, which is a fine thing to do.

The story of Liquid Paper and Bette Nesmith Graham is a story everyone can appreciate. It shows how a wonderful product came to market because of the cleverness and perseverance of its inventor. Perhaps you, too, have a clever idea that will spread like wildfire if only you can give it the kind of spark that Mrs. Graham gave to her product.*

---

*Based on an article from *The Wall Street Journal,* July 29, 1994, by Eric Morgenthaler.

2 USING RELATIVE PRONOUNS

The assignment in a university composition class was to write an essay with the title "The Teacher Who Influenced My Life the Most." Read this essay and select the correct word to introduce each adjective clause (write **0** *if no relative pronoun is needed).*

THE TEACHER WHO INFLUENCED MY LIFE THE MOST

School was always very important to me. Therefore, it is not surprising that the person ___who___ influenced my life the most was a teacher. In my twelve years of school,
1. (which / who)
I have had many teachers _____ I have admired greatly, but Mrs. Thompson,
2. (whom / which)
_____ was my French teacher in the tenth grade, is the teacher to
3. (that / who)
_____ I owe the most.
4. (whom / that)
Mrs. Thompson was an excellent teacher, and I really liked the way she taught the class. It was a class _____ I felt important. In this class, I was able to excel,
5. (where / which)
_____ helped me feel better about myself. Before I took this class, I was not the
6. (that / which)
kind of person _____ spoke up in groups. In fact, I was very quiet and did not
7. (whom / who)
socialize much. Because of the success _____ I had in this class, though, I
8. (whose / 0)
became more confident and at ease, something _____ also helped me to do
9. (when / which)
better in my other classes. I became a better student and a better person.

My family did not have a lot of money, and it looked like I wasn't going to be able to attend the university. However, Mrs. Thompson wrote strong letters recommending me for scholarships _____ I submitted along with the applications. In the end, I was
10. (whom / that)
able to get a scholarship to attend the university. After my acceptance arrived, Mrs. Thompson gave me advice regarding the classes I would take, as well as other academic matters. Those days at the beginning of my college career were difficult for me. They were days _____ I really needed someone's advice, and Mrs. Thompson came through
11. (when / which)
for me.

My final reason for choosing Mrs. Thompson is the subject to _____ she
12. (that / which)
introduced me. This was my first class in French, a language _____ I really liked
13. (that / whose)
to study. I enjoyed French so much that I then took Spanish the next year. I enjoyed

studying both languages and had excellent grades in all my language classes, an

accomplishment _____ has given me the idea of becoming a language teacher
⠀⠀⠀⠀⠀⠀⠀⠀⠀⠀⠀⠀⠀14. (0 / that)

myself. I can only hope that I will one day be able to teach as well as Mrs. Thompson,

_____ class had such a positive impact on my life.
15. (whom / whose)

3 USING RELATIVE PRONOUNS

Here are three job advertisements from the classified section of the newspaper. They are display ads, prominently set off from smaller ads. Each advertisement lists the skills and personality traits important for that job. Read the ads and select the correct word to introduce each adjective clause. Sometimes more than one answer is possible.

SECRETARY

Computer Future is looking for a person _____that_____ has the right skills for a
⠀⠀⠀⠀⠀⠀⠀⠀⠀⠀⠀⠀⠀⠀⠀⠀⠀⠀⠀⠀⠀⠀⠀⠀⠀1. (that / which / whom)

fast-paced, growing office. The current position, _____ is being announced
⠀⠀⠀⠀⠀⠀⠀⠀⠀⠀⠀⠀⠀⠀⠀⠀⠀⠀⠀⠀⠀⠀⠀⠀⠀2. (that / which, / whose)

here for the first time, is for a front office secretary. Thus, we are looking for a person who

can perform secretarial duties and work with the public. The ideal candidate for this

position is someone _____ can type at least 80 wpm and is comfortable with
⠀⠀⠀⠀⠀⠀⠀⠀⠀⠀⠀⠀⠀⠀3. (which / who / whom)

basic and advanced word processing programs. Our company stresses excellent customer

relations, so only those applicants _____ people skills are truly outstanding
⠀⠀⠀⠀⠀⠀⠀⠀⠀⠀⠀⠀⠀⠀⠀⠀⠀⠀⠀⠀4. (that / who / whose)

should apply; an outgoing personality is a requirement. We offer a very competitive

salary, full health insurance, a generous retirement plan, and opportunities for

professional growth, a package of _____ other companies can only
⠀⠀⠀⠀⠀⠀⠀⠀⠀⠀⠀⠀⠀⠀⠀⠀⠀⠀⠀5. (that / which / whom)

be envious. If you think you are the right person for this job, we urge you to apply today.

BILINGUAL TELEPHONE OPERATOR

A large multinational company seeks an energetic individual _____ has a
good telephone voice. Applicants _____ English and Spanish skills are
6. (which / who / whom)
7. (that / which / whose)
impeccable should call Mr. Wilford at 555-1417 to set up an appointment. In addition,
we seek someone _____ is familiar with a traditional switchboard but
8. (when / which / who)
_____ also knows how to operate a computer-driven switchboard. In
9. (where / which / who)
particular, applicants _____ are good with details are encouraged to apply.
10. (who / whom / whose)
The next two years will be a time _____ our company is expanding rapidly,
11. (when / which / who)
and similar jobs may be opening up in the very near future. Therefore, we urge all
interested persons to call for a job interview as soon as possible.

WEB PAGE DESIGNER

Our downtown office is looking for a creative person _____ can meet work
12. (where / who / whom)
deadlines. The ideal person for this job is someone _____ can translate a
13. (when / which / who)
client's ideas and needs into a dynamic Web page. We need a designer _____
14. (that / which / whose)
imagination can help turn mundane Web pages into innovative sites. In addition, we are
looking for a person _____ knows HTML and JAVA, programming
15. (who / whom / whose)
languages _____ our company uses extensively. If interested, you should
16. (that / where / whose)
submit a detailed resume, a small portfolio of previous Web creations, and three letters of
reference from clients for _____ you have worked during the last five years.
17. (which / who / whom)

4 USING RELATIVE PRONOUNS

Complete the article by filling in the blanks with appropriate relative pronouns from the box. Where more than one selection is possible, write all the possibilities, including 0 if no relative pronoun is needed.

who	which	that	where
whom	whose	when	0

Dr. Jennifer Wise has obtained a grant of $17 million for her research on the factors affecting the natural resistance __that / which / 0__ the human body has to cold
1.
viruses. Dr. Wise has investigated the common beliefs about catching colds to

_____ people have long subscribed—for example, the beliefs that colds come
2.
from sitting in places _____ there is a draft, not wearing warm enough
3.
clothing, and sitting near a person _____ is coughing and sneezing.
4.

She discredits all these ideas as having no merit but says that there are other factors

_____ actually contribute to catching a cold. For example, you can catch a
5.
cold from a person _____ you have been near just from touching him or her
6.
or something _____ he or she has touched, so it is important and effective to
7.
wash you hands frequently and well.

Additionally, not getting the rest _____ your body needs lowers resistance.
8.
People _____ sleep patterns don't provide them with enough deep sleep will
9.
more easily catch a cold than people _____ get enough rest. Deep sleep is
10.
especially important at times _____ people are under more stress than usual.
11.

As for treating the common cold: Nothing will cure it, but there are some palliative

steps _____ may be taken. You may take aspirin and other medications
12.
_____ act to relieve your discomfort, stay in bed if you can, drink plenty of
13.
liquids, and partake of the home remedy _____ has been around for
14.
centuries: the chicken soup _____ your mother makes.
15.

5 WRITING ADJECTIVE CLAUSES

Here is a summary of the information about the Meyers-Briggs Personality Inventory that is in your textbook. Below each blank is some information that you should rewrite in the form of an adjective clause. Sometimes more than one relative pronoun is possible. Remember that sometimes a relative pronoun may be omitted.

Of all the personality measurement instruments that exist today, perhaps the Meyers-Briggs Personality Inventory is the most well known. It is used extensively by human resources departments in an effort to help them understand the people who work in their company. What is the Meyers-Briggs Personality Inventory? Simply put, the Meyers-Briggs is a test <u>which / that indicates an individual's personality type</u>. According to this test, there
1. (The test indicates an individual's personality type.)
are four main dimensions, or categorizations, of personality. For each dimension, there are two categories.

The first dimension is a basic one: extrovert or introvert. An extrovert is a person
_____. An extrovert is not very comfortable
2. (This person feels energized around others.)
or productive being alone. In contrast, an introvert is a person
_____. An introvert feels most comfortable
3. (This person's energies are activated by being alone.)
when he or she is alone.

The second dimension is connected to how a person notices and remembers information. Some people in this category are referred to as sensors: those
_____. They rely on their past experiences
4. (Those people pay attention to details in the world.)
and knowledge of how science works to make objective determinations. Sensors are very practical people. In contrast, an intuitive is an individual
_____. Intuitives usually focus on
5. (The individual is more interested in relationships between people and things.)
what will probably be a successful move, mostly because they sense it is what people want. They are sensitive to other people's feelings and act accordingly.

The third personality dimension _____ is
6. (This test measures this dimension.)

that of thinker or feeler. Have you ever had a boss _____?
7. (Your boss made decisions objectively.)
Maybe you thought some of his decisions were cold or impersonal. Perhaps they were.

Perhaps your boss was a person _____
8. (The person has a primary way to reach a conclusion.)
was to determine what makes sense and what is logical. That boss was not a person

_____. Your boss was a thinker, not a feeler.
9. (The person took other people's feelings into consideration.)
A feeler, unlike that boss, makes decisions based on his or her own personal values and the

feelings _____ about the anticipated results
10. (He or she has feelings.)
of those decisions.

The final dimension deals with the type of environment in

_____: planned or unplanned. Judgers
11. (We prefer to live or work in this type of environment.)
are people _____; they judge, or anticipate,
12. (People prefer a planned and predictable environment.)
what is going to happen and try to live their lives in accordance with these plans.

In contrast, perceivers are more interested in keeping their options open. They want

to be able to respond to the needs of the situation and the moment

_____. Are you the kind of person
13. (They find themselves in the situation and the moment.)
_____, or do you prefer to take life one day
14. (The person's life must be planned in advance.)
at a time, and with some room for spontaneity?

A test such as the Meyers-Briggs may help determine what type of personality an

employee has and the spot _____. At the
15. (He should be placed here to most enhance the company.)
same time, you as an employee might benefit from a test like this because you might find

the place in _____
16. (You would be the happiest and most productive here.)

Unit 10

6 DISTINGUISHING BETWEEN IDENTIFYING AND NONIDENTIFYING CLAUSES

*Read the following sentences about the Moonrise Film Festival. Each of the sentences contains an adjective clause of either the identifying or nonidentifying type. For each, decide whether **A** or **B** describes the first sentence. Pay special attention to punctuation.*

1. Moviegoers, who appreciate fine films, were very satisfied with the Moonrise Film Festival this year.
   - **(A.)** Moviegoers in general appreciate fine films.
   - **B.** Only some moviegoers appreciate fine films.

2. Moviegoers who appreciate fine films were very satisfied with the Moonrise Film Festival this year.
   - **A.** Moviegoers in general appreciate fine films.
   - **B.** Only some moviegoers appreciate fine films.

3. The films, which were chosen for their artistry in cinematography, left vivid and lasting impressions.
   - **A.** The films in general left vivid and lasting impressions.
   - **B.** Only some films left vivid and lasting impressions.

4. The films that were chosen for their artistry in cinematography left vivid and lasting impressions.
   - **A.** The films in general left vivid and lasting impressions.
   - **B.** Only some films left vivid and lasting impressions.

5. Offbeat films brought critical acclaim to directors, who are normally very profit oriented.
   - **A.** Directors in general are normally very profit oriented.
   - **B.** Only some directors are normally very profit oriented.

6. Offbeat films brought critical acclaim to directors who are normally very profit oriented.
   - **A.** Directors in general are normally very profit oriented.
   - **B.** Only some directors are normally very profit oriented.

7. In the animation category, the audience was surprised and satisfied by Hollywood's new-style cartoons, which address serious social concerns.
   - **A.** Hollywood's new-style cartoons in general address social concerns.
   - **B.** Only some of Hollywood's new-style cartoons address social concerns.

8. In the animation category, the audience was surprised and satisfied by Hollywood's new-style cartoons that address serious social concerns.
   - **A.** Hollywood's new-style cartoons in general address social concerns.
   - **B.** Only some of Hollywood's new-style cartoons address social concerns.

9. The foreign entries, which were brilliantly directed, unfortunately may not succeed at the box office here.
   - **A.** The foreign entries in general were brilliantly directed.
   - **B.** Only some of the foreign entries were brilliantly directed.

10. Only the documentaries, which proved to be disappointing this year, represented a poor selection.
    A. The documentaries in general were a poor selection.
    B. Only some of the documentaries were a poor selection.
11. We hope to see further works from the new entrants from the African countries whose film industries are just emerging.
    A. The film industries in African countries in general are just emerging.
    B. The film industries in some African countries are just emerging.
12. If such excellence in selection and presentation continues, the Moonrise Film Festival will soon take its place among the film festivals of the world that rival Cannes.
    A. Film festivals in general rival Cannes.
    B. Only some film festivals rival Cannes.

7 EDITING

In the following article, find and correct the eighteen errors in the formation of the adjective clauses.

>   which
> One of the ways in ~~whom~~ people can be classified is by labeling them extroverts and introverts. However, there are other methods, some of them are now considered to have little scientific value, that people use to conveniently pigeonhole members of the human race.
>
>   For example, there is the division into mesomorphs, who are muscular; endomorphs, who tend to be fat; and ectomorphs, who are thin. The endomorph is stereotyped as a relaxed and unobsessive personality, whereas the ectomorph is stereotyped as a person whom is nervous and serious and whom rarely smiles.
>
>   A further facile division is made by defining people as Type A and Type B. Type A describes people to which everything is serious and who they are very ambitious and driving. Type A originally described people, usually middle-aged males, whom often suffered heart attacks. Type B, on the other hand, labels a rather passive, ambitionless person of that others frequently take advantage, and which is probably not a candidate for a heart attack.

(continued on next page)

Some people categorize human beings by the astrological sign that they were born under it. For example, a person who born between April 22 and May 21 is called a Taurus and is supposed to possess certain characteristics such as congeniality and tact. A person that born between June 22 and July 21 is a Cancer and is reputed to be stubborn but effective. There are twelve such categories, which encompass all the months of the year. Many people base their lives and relationships on the predictions made by astrologers.

One recent theory to categorize people is the theory of left-brained and right-brained people. Right-brained people, that are intuitive and romantic, are the artists and creative people of the world according to this theory. Left-brained people, who they are logical in their thinking, turn out to be mathematicians and scientists. According to this theory, people whose their abilities are not developed enough in the areas they would like can act to develop the side of the brain they want to improve it in order to better balance their personality.

All of these theories, which in themselves are too simplistic, are indeed unscientific. However, they have provided attractive and sometimes amusing solutions for people are looking for easy ways to understand the human race. Different theories of categorizing people, which it is always a difficult thing to do, will continue to come and go.

8 PERSONALIZATION

What is your concept of the ideal teacher and the ideal student? In the first paragraph, write a description of the kind of teacher you like best. In the second paragraph, imagine that you are a teacher. What kind of student do you prefer to have? Include some of the phrases from the boxes, appropriately finished with adjective clauses.

> The Ideal Teacher
> I like a teacher who . . .
> I would rather have a teacher whom . . .
> It's important to study with someone whose . . .
> The teacher would use instructional materials that . . .
> There will be times when . . .

> The Ideal Student
> The ideal student is a person . . .
> The ideal student is someone whose . . .
> This is a person for whom . . .
> The student will have free time that he or she . . .
> As a teacher, I would prefer to have students I . . .

UNIT 11
ADJECTIVE CLAUSES WITH QUANTIFIERS; ADJECTIVAL MODIFYING PHRASES

1 IDENTIFYING ADJECTIVE CLAUSES AND ADJECTIVE PHRASES

In the following passage, underline the adjective clauses and circle the adjective phrases.

The movie industry, (barely born before the turn of the century,) began producing silent films in the early 1900s. Filmmakers, learning how to fake prizefights, news events, and foreign settings, increased the length and variety of their films. Some of the early filmmakers, however, actually provided coverage of certain news events, <u>among which were the inauguration of President William McKinley and the action at the front in the Boer War.</u> Travelogues, many of which were filmed in remote parts of the world, became very popular, as did short science films, made with the aid of the microscope.

One of the important technical film pioneers was French magician Georges Méliès, credited with creating methods leading toward the development of special-effects movies. He used innovative techniques, examples of which include double exposure, mattes, slow and fast motion, animation, and miniature models. Through these techniques, he was able to create popular film fantasies, one of which was called *A Trip to the Moon* and influenced many subsequent filmmakers.

At the same time, filmmakers in England were developing fiction films shot outdoors, some of which involved chase scenes.

In 1903, Edwin S. Porter, a camera operator and director, made *The Great Train Robbery*, a movie showing different actions simultaneously. For some chase scenes, Porter mounted a camera in a car of a train. Along with bringing excitement and suspense to the movies, Porter firmly established the genre of the chase film, seen and loved even today.

Thus began the era of the silent film, changing the world forever.

2 FORMING ADJECTIVE CLAUSES WITH QUANTIFIERS

The following sentences present some interesting facts.* Complete these sentences by writing adjective clauses with quantifiers (or other expressions of quantity) + preposition + relative pronoun.

1. The average American's diet contains quite a bit of sodium, __most of which comes from processed food__.
   (most / come / from processed food)

2. In the past 20 years in Florida, insects, spiders, and alligators have caused 82 deaths, _____.
   (most / could / have / be avoided)

3. Hospital stays in Japan, _____,
   (half / be / longer than / 40 days)
   are far longer than hospital stays in the United States.

4. Americans today, _____, feel more
   (71 percent / think / people in power take advantage of others)
   victimized than did Americans in the past.

5. According to intelligence test results, stutterers, _____,
   (14 percent / achieve scores of over 130 on IQ tests)
   appear to be smarter than nonstutterers.

6. The hearing impaired, _____,
   (more than half / be / under 64 years of age)
   are a more diverse group than is sometimes thought.

7. Vegetables, _____,
   (all / yield / more nutrients when lightly cooked than when raw)
   can be microwaved, stir-fried, or quick-steamed.

8. Americans eat an average of 21.5 pounds per year of food between meals, _____.
   (much / be / junk food)

*The information is taken from *Health,* October 1993 and November–December 1994.

3 REDUCING ADJECTIVE CLAUSES TO ADJECTIVE PHRASES

Read the following descriptions of movies from a publication for TV viewers. Change the adjective clauses in parentheses to adjective phrases.

1. **Rocky II**

    In the sequel to this 1976 blockbuster, heavyweight Rocky Balboa gets a rematch in an action thriller, <u>written and directed by and again starring Sylvester Stallone</u>.
    (which was written and directed by and again stars Sylvester Stallone)

2. **Beauty and the Beast**

    This superlative animated musical from Disney tells of the romance between a beautiful young girl and a prince _____.
    (who has been transformed by a magic spell)

3. **The Rainmaker**

    Francis Ford Coppola has filmed a gripping account of a young lawyer

    _____
    (who takes on a big insurance company)
    and the obstacles he encounters.

4. **Lethal Weapon**

    This is an action thriller about a suicidal cop and his common-sense partner _____ a woman's plunge from a high-rise.
    (who are investigating)

5. **Titanic**

    The Oscar-winning blockbuster, _____
    (which stars Leonardo DiCaprio and Kate Winslet)
    as star-crossed lovers aboard the doomed ship, provides a moving story and amazing visual effects.

6. **Shakespeare in Love**

    This charming and fantastic tale, _____
    (which centers on a love affair)
    that WilliamShakespeare could have had, beautifully depicts Elizabethan England and the customs of the time.

7. The X-Files

FBI agents Mulder and Scully seek the truth about conspiracies, extra-terrestrials, and mysterious black ooze in this thriller mystery _____.
(which was adapted from the TV series)

8. Dumb and Dumber

In these hilarious adventures, two good-hearted but dumb fellows travel across the country to find the rightful owner of a briefcase _____.
(that is full of cash)

9. The Mask of Zorro

In the early nineteenth century, Zorro fights with his sword to right all wrongs. There are spills, thrills, romance, and laughter in this cape-and-mask escapade _____.
(that is sure to delight every member of the family)

10. Dave

Kevin Kline plays a dual role in this political satire about an employment agency owner _____.
(who has been enlisted to impersonate the president of the United States)

4 ADJECTIVE CLAUSES WITH QUANTIFIERS AND ADJECTIVE PHRASES

Read the following pairs of sentences. For each pair, combine the second sentence with the first one. Use an adjective phrase or, if the second sentence has a quantifier, an adjective clause with a quantifier.

CINEMA PUBS

If you want to see a movie but want to experience something different, try a cinema pub.

1. Cinema pubs are small. Being small gives you a more intimate relationship to the film.

   Cinema pubs are small, giving you a more intimate relationship to the film.

(continued on next page)

2. Instead of traditional seating, cinema pubs contain independent sections of tables and comfortable swivel chairs. This allows you to feel like you are in your own living room.

3. A server comes to each table before the movie begins and takes your order for food and beverages. Most of the servers are local college students.

4. The ambience in the theater is similar to that in a cabaret. In a cabaret, there is an intimate feeling.

5. In accordance with the cozy atmosphere, the cinema pubs show small films. Many of the small films are foreign.

6. Although you have come to the theater to see a movie, you will also find that the cinema pub is a good place. Here people like to socialize.

7. In fact, there are cinema pubs in certain areas. These cinema pubs are known as places where discriminating singles can go to meet each other.

8. The idea of the cinema pub is beginning to catch on in the United States. The idea of a cinema pub is already popular in the United Kingdom.

9. Cinema pubs show recent films in a relaxed atmosphere. This makes them a welcome alternative to huge and impersonal movie multiplexes.

_____

_____

10. For a change of pace, look in the newspaper for a cinema pub. A cinema pub may be in your city.

_____

_____

5 EDITING

Read the following passage on films after World War II. Find and correct the fifteen errors involving adjective clauses and phrases. Delete, fix, or replace words, but do not change punctuation or add words.

> After World War II, Europe was the center of important developments in filmmaking, which ~~they~~ strongly influenced motion pictures worldwide. In Italy, well-known movies, some of them were Rossellini's *Open City*, making in 1945, and De Sica's *Shoeshine* (1946) and *Bicycle Thief* (1948), established a trend toward realism in film. These directors weren't concerned with contrived plots or stories that produced for entertainment value alone; they took their cameras into the streets to make films showed the harshness of life in the years after the war. In the next decades, Federico Fellini, was an outstanding director, combined realistic plots with poetic imagery, symbolism, and philosophical ideas in now-classic films, the most famous of them is *La Strada*, which a movie ostensibly about circus people in the streets but really about the meaning of life.
>
> In France, a group of young filmmakers, calling the "New Wave," appeared during the 1950s. This group developed a new kind of focus, which stressed characterization rather than plot, and new camera and acting techniques, seeing in movies such as

(continued on next page)

Truffaut's *400 Blows*. In England, another group of filmmakers, was known as the "Angry Young Man" movement, developed a new realism. In Sweden, Ingmar Bergman used simple stories and allegories to look at complex philosophical and social issues, some of them are masterfully explored in *The Seventh Seal*. The Spaniard Luis Buñuel depicted social injustices and used surrealistic techniques, creating films like *Viridiana*.

Postwar developments in filmmaking were not limited to Western Europe. The Japanese director Akira Kurosawa, was the first Asian filmmaker to have a significant influence in Europe, made *Rashomon* in 1950. Movies from India, like Satyajit Ray's *Panther Panchali*, showed us life on the subcontinent. Even in Russia, where filmmaking was under state control, it was possible to make movies like *The Cranes Are Flying*, portray the problems of the individual. Russian directors also made films based on literary classics, included Shakespeare's plays and Tolstoi's monumental historical novel, *War and Peace*.

In summary, in the decades after World War II, filmmaking turned in new directions, as shown by a wide range of movies from around the world, many of them focused on the meaning of life and how to interpret it.

6 PERSONALIZATION

What was the best movie that you have ever seen? What can you remember about it? Write a short essay about the movie. Begin with this sentence: **One of my favorite movies is** _____.
Include some of the phrases from the box.

> I liked the movie for a number of reasons, some of which are . . .
> The movie had some good actors, including . . .
> The movie had some really exciting (funny) scenes, examples of which are . . .
> I remember the scene taking place . . .
> There was an exciting plot, involving . . .
> The movie had an interesting ending, resulting in . . .
> The director was _____, also known for directing . . .
> I like his (her) movies, all of which . . .
> The movie won some awards, including . . .
> I would have no trouble recommending this movie, one of the . . .
> Perhaps this movie will be shown again soon, in which case . . .

PART V PASSIVE VOICE

UNIT 12

THE PASSIVE: REVIEW AND EXPANSION

1 IDENTIFYING PASSIVE CONSTRUCTIONS

Read the following excerpts about local crime from the newspaper. Underline the twenty-one passive constructions.

Storyville School Vandalized
STORYVILLE — Storyville's Country Day School <u>was vandalized</u> last weekend. Some of the items that were stolen from the school were five computers, a CD player, and sports equipment, the value of which is approximately $11,000. No clues were left by the thieves, and as of this morning, information as to their identity was still being sought by police. School officials could not be contacted for comment.

Restaurant Burglarized After Hours
MARGARITAVILLE — The Margaritaville Cantina was burglarized just before dawn on Sunday morning. Police found that the lock on the back door had been altered prior to the burglary. This is the third time since November that restaurants in the 3400 block of Aspen Avenue have been broken into. Police Chief Bill Griffin stated that a full investigation is being made and that he expects that the perpetrators will be arrested shortly. The owner of the restaurant states that he is going to have a better alarm system installed.

Barking Dog Removed to Shelter
WESTVIEW — A barking dog that belongs to a family in the 400 block of Pear Tree Street is the source of problems between neighbors. Sunday afternoon a complaint was filed with police by next-door neighbors, who claim that their peace is always being disturbed by the dog's constant barking. They state that they should not be forced to endure the noise, and they want to have the dog removed from the property. The owners are out of town and cannot be reached. The dog is being cared for temporarily at the City Animal Shelter.

Cash Register Damaged, Waiter Is Fired
NORTHSIDE — An upset waiter at Pop's Place smashed the computer screen of a restaurant cash register after midnight on Wednesday. The waiter, 22, was fired but not arrested. His manager wanted to have the incident documented by police and to have the alleged offender barred from the premises in the future. The damage is estimated at $1,100.

2 USING ACTIVE AND PASSIVE CONSTRUCTIONS

*Complete the following information from travel brochures by putting the verbs in parentheses into either active or passive constructions. Use a form of **be** in the passive constructions.*

TRAVEL, INC.

CANCUN

Here, amid the ruins of the ancient Mayas, you ____will find____ the world's
                                              1. (will / find)
most beautiful beaches and clear blue waters. You _____ by the
                                                  2. (will / caress)
gentle breezes as you _____ languidly around the pool or on the
                      3. (laze)
white sand. At night, after you _____ the sensuous Yucatán cuisine,
                                4. (savor)
you _____ by the strolling Mariachi musicians.
    5. (will / thrill)

PUERTO RICO

Experience the pleasures of Puerto Rico. Cruise the crystal-clear waters of the Atlantic, dive into the Caribbean, and enjoy the fishing and nighttime swimming. The galleries and shops of cobblestoned Old San Juan _____, and its
                                                         6. (must / see)
restaurants _____. Both Spanish and English _____
            7. (must / enjoy)   8. (speak)
here.

HAWAII

You _____ by the astonishing array of luxurious tropical
    9. (will / delight)
products, from sun-ripened papayas to macadamia nuts and orchids. Hawaii
_____ long ago by Polynesians, who _____ by the
10. (settle)   11. (enchant)
beauty and lushness of the islands and therefore never _____ them.
                                                        12. (leave)
You won't want to leave either!

(continued on next page)

JAMAICA

Here in the land of luxurious vegetation, cool mountains, and gorgeous beaches, you _____ the original reggae and calypso music. Dance to the steel
    13. (can / experience)
bands and enjoy the beautiful weather, the waterfalls, and the hospitality of people

who _____ a special elegant English. In this romantic spot in the
      14. (speak)
Caribbean, you _____ by everything around you.
                15. (will / enchant)

BERMUDA

This perfect gem in the Atlantic, which _____ by England, retains
                                        16. (colonize)
its British traditions and is considered the most quietly charming island in the

Western Hemisphere. Automobiles _____ in much of Bermuda;
                                 17. (allow / not)
bicycles and motor scooters _____ at reasonable rates.
                             18. (may / rent)
There are many excellent shopping opportunities, especially for articles that

_____ from the United Kingdom.
  19. (import)

3 USING PASSIVE CONSTRUCTIONS

*In the following letter to her parents, a young space exobiologist writes home from Mars in 2025. Complete the letter with passive constructions with **be** and the verbs in parentheses. Some items may have additional correct answers.*

Dear Mom and Dad:

This is a pretty good place to be on my first job. Just think, a year ago I was still writing papers and worrying about my dissertation, and now here I am using my *cooking* skills on Mars, along with my exobiology degree. I'll bet you never thought I ___would actually be paid___ for doing things most people think of as hobbies
   1. (would / actually / pay)
(gardening and cooking) and that what I studied in college

_____ in such a productive and useful manner.
  2. (would / actually / employ)

Life _____ quite well here using the original plants that
      3. (sustain)

_____ up with us. The plants
_____4. (send)_____

_____ here in growth chambers where environmental
_____5. (maintain)_____
conditions—like lighting, nutrient supply, temperature, and humidity—

_____ by computer. Crops _____
___6. (must control)___   ___7. (cannot grow)___
using sunlight, as here on Mars sunlight is available for only half of each rotation period,

and in addition, sometimes the sun _____ for months at a
                                      ___8. (obscure)___
time by the giant dust storms we have on Mars. Everything _____
                                                            ___9. (has to do)___
efficiently here. There is no waste, as all the waste that _____
                                                            ___10. (has / produce)___
from plants as well as from humans _____ to nourish the next
                                      ___11. (recycle)___
generation of growth. Everything _____ up. It's so interesting
                                  ___12. (get / use)___
to see how the resources of power and space _____ and
                                                ___13. (have / utilize)___
_____.
___14. (maximize)___

You would be very proud of my culinary creativity in using the vegetables. I'm

particularly glad to have tomatoes, which _____ to be like
                                             ___15. (develop)___
those famous New Jersey tomatoes. I _____ among our
                                      ___16. (know)___
group here for my delicious salads, which _____ with the
                                             ___17. (make)___
tomatoes, along with potatoes, black-eyed peas, and peanuts. As you know, no meat or

fish of any kind _____ here, only vegetables. Even the
                  ___18. (find)___
water comes from plants. We put in our orders for water one day ahead of time, and

we _____ by a special water-collecting crew every morning.
   ___19. (have / it / collect)___
The water _____ through plant materials, too, and believe
           ___20. (filter)___
it or not, it is delicious!

I hope you'll be able to visit me before the end of the year. A beautiful new hotel

_____ now and _____ in July.
___21. (build)___   ___22. (will / complete)___
Please call me on Sunday as usual.

Your loving daughter,

Eliza

Unit 12

4 RECOGNIZING AND WRITING PASSIVE CAUSITIVES WITH *HAVE*

"Action Line" is a newspaper column that helps readers with problems. Underline passive causatives in these readers' letters to "Action Line." (Each letter has one or more causatives.) Then complete the solutions by changing the phrase in parentheses into a passive causative with **have**.

1. My grandparents have lived in their apartment building for nearly thirty years. Now they have termites, and the landlord is refusing to <u>have the building treated</u> by professional exterminators. He says that he can't afford it, so he's just having their apartment sprayed. I know that's not enough. What can be done?

    Solution: Action Line did it. We called the Department of Business Regulations, which handles complaints like yours, and they
    _____have already had the landlord investigated_____.
    (have / already / investigate the landlord)
    If the landlord doesn't properly get rid of the termites by the 15th of next month, he will be fined $1,000.

2. I have a Picky eight-track tape player. It used to work fine, but since the last snowstorm, it's been making a lot of noise. My nephew asked me if I had ever had the heads of the tape player cleaned. I said no. Is that what I should do?

    Solution: Les Garth, owner of The Audio Place, told Action Line that he doesn't recommend cleaning the heads of tape players like yours. He said you
    _____,
    (should / transfer the tapes to regular cassettes)
    which he can do for you for $7.95 each.

3. I had some furniture sent to my house from Modella Furniture Company in North Carolina. The furniture arrived, but a leg on the table had broken off. I wrote to the company and spoke to a secretary there on the phone, but it has been two months now and nothing has been done. What can you do, Action Line?

    Solution: Action Line was able to get through to the president of the company. We arranged to _____,
    (an insurance adjuster look at your table)
    and Modella has agreed to pay for a replacement table if necessary.

4. I took my new, very expensive formal gown to Alfie's Alterations to have it shortened. It was shortened, all right! When I got it back, the skirt was five inches above my knees! Alfie's apologized and gave me credit to have future alterations done there, but this doesn't compensate me for the hundreds of dollars I spent on the dress, which is now ruined. Action Line, can something be done?

Solution: Yes, it already has been done. Action Line sent a representative to Alfie's. Alfie Brown, the owner, said to replace the dress and to

_____.
(send the bill to him)

5. My car is eleven years old and has been running smoothly all this time. Then last month it began stalling. I have had it checked by my mechanic, and he wasn't able to fix it. I am at my wits' end, because I love this car. Any suggestions, Action Line?

Solution: Action Line has contacted the manufacturer. They tell us that an eleven-year-old car is, of course, under no warranty, but since they want their customers to be happy, they said to take it to the nearest dealer, where they _____, if it's at all possible.
(will / fix the problem)

6. Our thirteen-year-old son volunteers at a shelter for homeless people. This work is very important to him. The trouble is that both my wife and I work full time and we live in a rural area with inadequate public transportation. The shelter had had a car sent for him each day but can no longer do so. Any suggestions, Action Line?

Solution: Action Line called the volunteer group Side-by-Side Rides. They pick up deserving people like your son and take them where they need to go. You can call the group at 555-0965 and arrange to

_____.
(pick up your son)

5 USING PASSIVE CONSTRUCTIONS WITH GET

*Read the following response from Marco to his friend Ricardo. Complete the letter with passive constructions with **get** and the indicated verbs.*

Dear Ricardo,

I'm sorry to hear that you _____got hit_____ by money problems, although it
             1. (hit)
sounds like some of them are your own fault. I'm also sorry that I won't be able to help you. I've got some problems of my own.

Last week, I had to _____. It suddenly refused to go—right in the middle
                    2. (my car / fix)
of rush hour traffic! After two hours, it finally _____ by a tow truck to
                                                  3. (tow)
a repair shop. The next day my car was running fine again. But I _____
                                                                   4. (charge)
$450 for the repair.

This week has been even worse. On Monday, someone broke into my apartment. All my
good things _____: my TV, my sound system, and even my new bicycle.
            5. (steal)
In the middle of all this, I also _____ by Lisa, the girl I wrote you about.
                                   6. (dump)
"Get dumped" is an expression that means she doesn't want to go out with me anymore.
At least I think she doesn't.

About your situation: I think you should get a night job. You really need the money, and
working will keep you out of trouble. If you can _____ by a hotel chain,
                                                  7. (hire)
for example, you might have the beginnings of a really good managerial job later. I hear
that they like to hire young people to work at night. If the person does well, he often
_____ to stay on for a real job. I think you would be great at it.
   8. (ask)
All you have to do is behave yourself and make sure you don't _____
                                                                9. (fire)
because of doing something stupid.

Hopefully, things will be better for both of us soon.

                                                              Marco

6 CHANGING ACTIVE CONSTRUCTIONS TO PASSIVE CONSTRUCTIONS

Improve the writing style in the following descriptions of ingredients used in Mexican cooking by changing the underlined sentences and clauses from active constructions to passive constructions. For each sentence where there is a change, write the full sentence, keeping the same tense and modal auxiliaries. Do not use **people** *or other indefinite words in your* **by** *phrases in your passive sentences.*

1. **Sesame seeds** People use sesame seeds in Mexican sauces.
   You can toast them easily. The Spanish introduced them to Mexico.
   And before that, the Moors had brought them to Spain.

   a. Sesame seeds are used in Mexican sauces.

   b. _____

   c. _____

   d. _____

2. **Pepitas (pumpkin seeds)** People grind pepitas for use in sauces.
   People also eat them whole. Even if people have ground them, the sauce has a rough texture. People have used pepitas since pre-Columbian times.

   a. _____

   b. _____

   c. _____

   d. _____

3. **Chorizo** Chorizo is similar in appearance to a sausage. In Mexico, people make it of unsmoked meat and spices. In Spain, people smoke the meat.

   a. _____

   b. _____

4. **Jicama** Jicama is a brown-skinned root vegetable with a white, crisp flesh similar to that of a radish. Street vendors in Mexico sell jicama in thick slices that somebody has sprinkled with salt, lime juice, and chili powder.

   a. _____

(continued on next page)

Unit 12

5. **Avocados** People consider avocados a true delicacy. If they are hard,
   <u>a.</u>
   somebody should allow them to ripen. People make guacamole from avocados.
   <u>b.</u>   <u>c.</u>
   People also use avocados in salads and as a garnish.
   <u>d.</u>

   a. _____
   b. _____
   c. _____
   d. _____

6. **Banana leaves** People steam meat in little packets of banana leaves.
   <u>a.</u>
   First, you must soften them over a flame. Then,
   <u>b.</u>
   you wrap the meat and other ingredients in them.
   <u>c.</u>

   a. _____
   b. _____
   c. _____

7. **Plantains** These look like bananas but are larger and firmer.

   People cook them in various ways, including deep-frying and baking.
   <u>a.</u>
   You may substitute firm green bananas.
   <u>b.</u>

   a. _____
   b. _____

8. **Tortillas** These are round and look like pancakes. People can eat them with any meal.
   <u>a.</u>
   People make them from corn or wheat flour.
   <u>b.</u>
   People can now find frozen tortillas in supermarkets.
   <u>c.</u>

   a. _____
   b. _____
   c. _____

9. **Chilies** People use chilies to season many different dishes. There are various
   <u>a.</u>
   kinds of chilies. In degree of spiciness, they range from very mild to very hot.
   Humans have consumed chili-seasoned foods for more than 8,000 years.
   <u>b.</u>

   a. _____
   b. _____

10. **Corn** <u>People use corn widely in Mexico</u>. In Mexican cooking,
a.
<u>people waste no part of the corn</u>. <u>People use the ears, husks,</u>
b.   c.
<u>silk, and kernels in different ways</u>. This was the first plant
<u>that people cultivated in Mexico</u>. Archaeologists found evidence
d.
that dates it to 5000 B.C.

a. _____

b. _____

c. _____

d. _____

7 EDITING

Read the following student paper. Find and correct the ten errors in the use of passives.

THE BERMUDA TRIANGLE MYSTERY

                              explained
A famous mystery that has never been really ~~explain~~ is that of the Devil's Triangle, which also known as the Bermuda Triangle. These names refer to an area in the Atlantic Ocean where, over a period of centuries, many mysterious disappearances of ships and airplanes have been occurred. A satisfactory explanation of the disappearances has never found. While many theories about turbulence and other atmospheric disturbances have been proposing, no meteorologic peculiarities about the area have proven. Violent storms and downward air currents have frequently been record there, but nothing has been find outside the limits of real and possible weather conditions.

   Boundaries of the triangle usually are form by drawing an imaginary line from Melbourne, Florida, to Bermuda to Puerto Rico and back to Florida. However, larger boundaries draw by some writers who want to treat far-ranging disappearances as part of the Bermuda Triangle mystery.

8 PERSONALIZATION

What person outside your family has played an important part in your life? Write something about how this person has influenced you. Include some of the phrases from the box.

> I have been most influenced by . . .
> I was helped by _____ to . . .
> I was persuaded by _____ to . . .
> I was taught by _____ to . . .
> My values were formed because . . .
> I am still inspired by _____, especially by the way he/she . . .
> His/Her influence can be seen in . . .
> _____ will always be remembered by me for . . .

REPORTING IDEAS AND FACTS WITH PASSIVES

UNIT 13

1 IDENTIFYING PASSIVE CONSTRUCTIONS

Read this magazine article. Underline the passive constructions which report ideas and facts.

Stay Well Magazine

It <u>used to be thought</u> that people caught colds by sitting in drafts, going out in cold weather, or going from hot to cold temperatures quickly. But now these ideas are believed to be false. It is now known that colds spread only by viruses transmitted from one person to another. Surprisingly, it is not the fact of being near an infected person that causes another person to catch a cold; it is now understood that transmission of viruses occurs most frequently when healthy people touch an object that the infected person has recently touched, such as a doorknob or a telephone, and then touch their own noses or mouths without having washed their hands well.

Colds are regarded as bothersome, but often unavoidable. Most of the time, the symptoms—a sore throat, runny nose, sneezing, mild cough, and headache—run their course and disappear within a week, with or without treatment. Antibiotics are assumed to be of no use whatsoever in combating a cold.

Chicken soup has been found to help relieve the symptoms of a cold by opening up the breathing passages and relieving the congestion. For many years, the power of chicken soup had been

(continued on next page)

considered just an old wives' tale, but recently, scientific research was reported in the *New England Journal of Medicine* showing that the custom of taking chicken soup for a cold actually is effective in relieving its symptoms.

For treatment of a cold, then, it is recommended that a person ease his or her symptoms by drinking plenty of fluids, especially hot fluids, and getting extra rest. To alleviate the general discomfort medically, aspirin and ibuprofen are known to help; to ease the congestion and runny nose, antihistamines and decongestants are suggested.

As the old saying goes, an ounce of prevention is worth a pound of cure. That is, measures to avoid catching the cold virus are considered more effective than measures to get rid of it.

2 USING PASSIVES TO REPORT IDEAS

Read the following conversation between Dr. Carl Clark, the host of a radio talk show, "Raising the Modern Child," and Margaret, a grandparent who is calling the show for advice. Complete the sentences with passive constructions, using the indicated verbs in a correct tense.

CALLER: I used to hear the saying that "children should be seen and not heard." I was brought up that way and tried to bring up my children that way. Now I see my daughter permitting her children to do almost anything they want. Isn't this kind of permissiveness bad?

DR. CLARK: The idea that children should be seen and not heard <u>used to be considered</u>
　　　　　　　　　　　　　　　　　　　　　　　　　　　　　　　1. (used to / consider)
one of the basic principles for raising children. However, in the modern world, this idea _____ to have made much trouble by
　　　　　　　　　　2. (believe)
causing neurosis in children. It _____ that by making
　　　　　　　　　　　　　　　　3. (previously / think)
children behave quietly, stifling all their feelings, and just keeping them pretty to look at, the children would grow up to be polite, law-abiding citizens. While this is true to a large extent in many cases, now it _____
　　　　　　　　　　　　　　　　　　　　　　　　　　　　　4. (understand)

that imposing too many restrictions will inhibit the child too much and can cause serious psychological problems.

CALLER: But, Carl, doesn't letting a child always have his or her own way spoil the child?

DR. CLARK: Of course, not setting limits on a child's behavior is not good training. But, it _____ that constantly thwarting children and not
5. (well / know)
permitting them to express their feelings can lead to serious frustration and possibly non-productive or antisocial behavior patterns. The trick is to lead children firmly and correct them gently.

CALLER: I really can't agree with you, Doctor. I believe that if you spare the rod, you spoil the child. Children need punishment.

DR. CLARK: You _____ by many as correct, Margaret. But let me
6. (would / perceive)
warn you: It _____ by all child-rearing experts these
7. (widely / confirm)
days that you MUST spare the rod. At the same time, you should not spoil the child. It _____ for quite some time now that children
8. (have / well / establish)
must be able to express themselves, but they must be taught to do so in a socially acceptable way.

CALLER: Well, Carl, you _____ by everyone to be the big expert,
9. (know)
but I am sorry, I just disagree with what you're telling me.

DR. CLARK: Well, Margaret, for many years now my kind of thinking _____ to be correct. You are entitled to have your
10. (consider)
opinion. But don't worry about your grandchildren. What your daughter is doing _____ to be the right thing.
11. (can / assume)

3 USING PASSIVES TO REPORT IDEAS

Read the following article. Fill in the blanks with passive constructions, using the indicated verbs.

Until recently, backgammon __was regarded__ in America as an exotic, unfamiliar
                                1. (regard)
game. Today, backgammon _____ to be the fastest-growing game in
                              2. (believe)
popularity, and it _____ to have millions of dedicated players, hundreds
                      3. (claim)
of clubs, and an international circuit of major tournaments. Backgammon experts

_____ to command lesson fees of over $150 per hour now.
   4. (report)

How old is backgammon? Historians are not sure. It _____ exactly
                                                        5. (not / know)
when the game originated, but when archaeologists excavated the ancient Sumerian city

of Ur, they found in the royal cemetery five game boards that closely resembled early

backgammon boards; from this, it _____ that the game existed five
                                      6. (now / assume)
thousand years ago. Similar to the game boards unearthed at Ur was a board discovered

among the treasures in the tomb of the Egyptian king Tutankhamen, from around 1500

B.C. Backgammon _____ to have been popular among the common
                    7. (also / think)
Egyptians, because ancient Egyptian wall paintings show people playing a table game.

Oddly enough, the Spanish explorer Francisco Pizarro in the early sixteenth century

described the Aztecs in Mexico playing a game remarkably like the Egyptians' game. After

this similarity had been established, it _____ that the early people of
                                            8. (conjecture)
the Americas might have migrated to the Western Hemisphere from areas near Egypt.

The ancient Greeks and Romans, too, _____ to have played a game like
                                         9. (now / believe)
backgammon. Plato commented on its popularity, and it _____ by those
                                                           10. (say)
who study ancient Greece that he might have played it himself. It _____
                                                                      11. (know)
that *tabulae*, a Roman version of the game, was popular in Pompeii, because a *tabulae*

board was found in the courtyard of almost every villa in the ruins there.

We know quite a bit about backgammon in the eighteenth century. For example,

backgammon _____ to have been popular among clergymen and
                12. (know)

physicians in Europe, and in America, Thomas Jefferson _____ by some
                                                        13. (now / think)
scholars to have played it for relaxation during the time when he was writing the
Declaration of Independence.

Backgammon's popularity has risen and fallen through the ages. It _____
                                                                  14. (can / safely / assume)
that its popularity will fall and rise again.*

*Based on Richard B. Manchester, *Amazing Facts* (New York: Bristol Park Books, 1991).

4 EDITING

Read the following first draft of an article. Find and correct the twenty-four errors in all forms of passives, including to report ideas.

                              declared
In Washington yesterday, it was ~~declaring~~ by an advisory panel to the Senate that nicotine is definitely an addictive drug. This formal declaration believes to go further than any previous one in officially condemning the use of tobacco, and it may be the first step toward government regulation of tobacco distribution.

For many years now, the dangers of cigarettes been recognized. It is no longer consider sophisticated to smoke, and in fact, people who do so are now considering unwise. More and more, smoking in public places has eliminated by local and state laws. Smoking now prohibited in many places: in hospitals, in government buildings, in business offices, and on domestic flights. While gigantic strides have made in the war against smoking, among serious non-smokers it is still thinking that enough hasn't been doing yet. These non-smokers believe that almost all smoking should be illegal, even in some private homes. Smoking in areas where there are children is considering by them to be a form of child abuse. In addition, precisely because of the addictive qualities of tobacco, they want to eliminate children's access to it.

Not everyone shares these beliefs. Although it has now been establishing that the effects of smoking are in fact disastrous, it also know that many citizens deeply resent

(continued on next page)

being told what to do. It feels by militant smokers that the government might be able to exert too much control over people's lives by having the ability to legislate the use of tobacco. If any laws to restrict smoking further are going to be proposed, it is assumes that the militant smokers will fight hard against them.

In addition, the problems of enforcing the no-smoking laws are regard as very difficult. Very few violators fined, and even fewer jailed. Understandably, the police don't want to spend their time apprehending an illegal smoker when three blocks away a robbery may be taking place and a police officer will need.

The antismokers have become optimistic, however. A public awareness about the evils of smoking now exists, and smoking not permitted in many places anymore. Programs and clinics have established all over to help people stop smoking. Children are being educating to be aware of the dangers of smoking. It is conjecturing that by the year 2010, smoking will been almost eliminated.

5 PERSONALIZATION

What strange, often-told stories have you heard of? Do you know mysteries like that of the Bermuda Triangle? Stories of supernatural creatures such as witches, vampires, and ghosts? Superstitions about things that bring bad luck or things that bring good luck? Write a paragraph about what people say about a mystery, a supernatural creature, or several superstitions. Include some of the phrases from the box.

It is said that . . .	. . . are said to . . .
It is thought that . . .	. . . are thought to . . .
It is believed that . . .	. . . are believed to . . .
It is claimed that . . .	. . . are claimed to . . .

Answer Key

Note: In this answer key, where the contracted form is given, the full form is also correct, and where the full form is given, the contracted form is also correct.

PART I TENSE AND TIME

UNIT 1 PRESENT AND FUTURE TIME

1

2. are going to have
3. 'll be walking
4. 'll go
5. will have
6. will be walking
7. will have grown
8. will be having
9. will be
10. am thinking
11. have
12. 's going to buy
13. doesn't sing
14. 's going to buy
15. are you crying

2

2. 1, 2
3. 2, 1
4. 2, 1
5. 2, 1
6. 2, 1
7. 2, 1
8. 1, 2

3

I don't think P
'm sending P
'll get F
if I put F
that will give F
the ad appears F
I will have lost F
A new issue is coming out F
've missed P ✓
The ad will appear F
which comes out F
'll be waiting for F
'm looking for P
've belonged P ✓
've lived P ✓
loved P ✓
'm looking for P

4

2. greet
3. board
4. will feel
5. venture
6. explore
7. are
8. won't want
9. will have been experiencing
10. return
11. will have experienced

5

2. are
3. will be/is going to be
4. will receive/is going to receive
5. is
6. go
7. graduate/have graduated
8. is going to star/will star/is starring
9. will be/is going to be
10. starts
11. have been going
12. will have/are going to have
13. get
14. will we all be doing
15. will have been working
16. (will have been) studying
17. (will have been) keeping
18. will have

6

has given → have given/have been giving/give
I study → I am studying
I do well → I have been doing well/am doing well
people are speaking → people speak
food is not being → food is not
it's raining → it rains
I didn't meet → I haven't met
I hadn't been having → I haven't been having/I'm not having
making me feel good → makes me feel good
I'm very happy → I'll be very happy

Answer Key

I will leave → I leave
will had been studying → will have been studying
will have learn → will have learned
I have finished → I will have finished
I'll work → I'll be working
I learn → I will learn

7

(Answers will vary.)

UNIT 2 PAST TIME

1

2. came
3. began
4. had begun
5. have been arriving
6. would settle
7. came
8. have sprung
9. used to be
10. had come
11. spread
12. would assimilate
13. has occurred

2

2. 2, 1
3. 2, 1
4. 1, 2
5. 2, 1
6. 1, 2
7. 1, 2
8. 2, 1
9. 2, 1
10. 1, 2

3

2. learned
3. had been working
4. came
5. hadn't passed
6. was studying
7. worked
8. had passed
9. established
10. retired
11. had been practicing
12. used to contribute
13. has been
14. got
15. had been taking
16. got
17. would take
18. have been having
19. got
20. have been working
21. used to work
22. was working
23. met
24. became
25. arrived
26. hadn't expected
27. would succeed

4

2. fix
3. is
4. call
5. hasn't
6. promises
7. buy
8. didn't
9. making
10. has
11. was going to
12. take
13. will

5

2. died/had died
3. continued
4. was attending
5. introduced
6. lost
7. met
8. had begun
9. would go/used to go/went
10. sent
11. would like
12. received
13. called
14. invited
15. have spent
16. have traveled
17. had been

6

hadn't thought → didn't think
have already decided → had already decided
didn't had → didn't have
will not give → would not give
has been solving → had been solving
don't believe → didn't believe
will be → would be
were moving → had moved/moved
is → was
study → were studying
already mastered → had already mastered
had become → became
has been studying → had been studying
has graduated → graduated
were realizing → realized
used to walking → used to walk/would walk
were thinking → thought
has been → was

7

(Answers will vary.)

UNIT 3 PAST, PRESENT, AND FUTURE

1

2. don't have
3. used to stay
4. are seeing
5. has developed
6. weighs
7. means
8. is resting
9. place
10. recognizes
11. will chase
12. have programmed
13. moves
14. download
15. doesn't fetch
16. doesn't jump
17. have already developed
18. makes
19. uses
20. activates
21. have
22. don't involve
23. don't break
24. don't require
25. experience

Answer Key

❷

2. have portrayed
3. has been
4. started
5. had appeared
6. allowed
7. gave
8. had never accomplished
9. entertained
10. starred
11. did not look
12. helped
13. see
14. will have increased
15. will be
16. will be
17. will dispense
18. believe
19. will perform
20. will take over/will have taken over
21. used to seem

❸

2. have finished
3. means
4. are embarking
5. were you doing
6. had just finished
7. were probably relaxing
8. were probably looking
9. have gone
10. you'll be doing
11. will be working
12. will remember
13. will have benefited
14. began
15. had been raising
16. was working
17. possessed
18. was working
19. used to be
20. would fall
21. thought
22. would have to
23. got
24. is graduating
25. has
26. graduates
27. used to make
28. gets
29. will have been studying
30. will have succeeded
31. are
32. will have
33. have successfully completed
34. will reach

❹

2. b	6. b	10. d	14. d
3. d	7. a	11. b	
4. d	8. c	12. b	
5. a	9. c	13. d	

❺

2. are going to hear/will hear/hear/will be hearing/are hearing
3. used to be/was
4. has telephoned
5. left
6. told
7. testified
8. used to steal/would steal/stole
9. stated
10. had gone/went
11. had been playing
12. stopped
13. was hurting
14. found
15. had seen/saw
16. were talking
17. went
18. have been waiting
19. is saying
20. seems
21. will continue/is going to continue
22. has requested
23. will prove/is going to prove
24. will be watching/are going to be watching
25. will have already learned

❻

'm missing → miss
am → have been
do → am doing
have → have had
gets → will get
aren't seeming → don't seem
being → am
is tasting → tastes
doesn't has → doesn't have
are eating → eat
're serving → serve
do → are doing
work → are working
enjoy → are enjoying
is having → has
're having → have
have filled → fill
are needing → need
have been → will have been

❼

(Answers will vary.)

PART II MODALS

UNIT 4 MODALS: NECESSITY

1
2. should
3. doesn't have to
4. should
5. don't have to
6. have to
7. must
8. should
9. ought to
10. were supposed to
11. had to
12. should have

2
2. b
3. b
4. c
5. c
6. c
7. a
8. b
9. b
10. a

3
2. must write
3. has to catch
4. should say
5. should continue
6. might say
7. could invent
8. can list
9. should make
10. got to meet
11. might be

4
2. should
3. can't
4. can
5. don't have to
6. can
7. should
8. shouldn't
9. should
10. should
11. can
12. don't have to
13. must
14. might/could
15. might/could
16. might/could
17. might/could
18. should
19. better not

5
2. should I buy
3. could find
4. have to pay
5. Should I have bought
6. had better be
7. didn't have to bring
8. was supposed to do
9. are supposed to say
10. will have to come
11. should have brought
12. could have brought
13. could have learned
14. could have been

6
can't to → can't
have to find → had to find
might to do → might do
could send → C
must just send → might just send
will send → would send
Am I supposed to get → C
haven't to do → don't have to
ought to do → C
could easily have forgotten → C
must have asked → should have asked
must not have → does not need

7
(Answers will vary.)

UNIT 5 MODALS: CERTAINTY

1
2. have cheated
3. be very angry; be in jail
4. be operative
5. speak Japanese
6. be very effective
7. want to anger the voters
8. have won a big victory
9. like skiing; not have snowed recently

2
2. can't
3. might; might
4. must; Seoul, Tokyo, and Mexico City
5. could; could
6. should; China
7. must; Norway
8. has to; Cuba
9. might; might
10. must; Finland

3
2. must
3. might
4. must
5. could
6. must
7. may
8. could
9. might
10. must
11. must
12. might
13. may not
14. can't
15. must not
16. should

4
2. a
3. a
4. b
5. a
6. a
7. b
8. a
9. b
10. b

5

2. must be
3. couldn't eat
4. must be
5. might make
6. ought to be/should be
7. ought to be/should be
8. could have eaten
9. can still do
10. must be
11. should take
12. could have ordered

6

(Some answers may vary.)

2. False Georgia is only two years old. / A baby couldn't have committed a murder.
3. True It's possible. / We don't have any information about the murder weapon. / It could have been a knife.
4. True It's possible. She was envious of the money, so she had a motive.
5. False We have no reason to make this conclusion. / She's probably too old to have the strength to kill anyone. / She was asleep at the time.
6. True He loved his brother, so it is very unlikely that he killed him.
7. False We have no information about the murder weapon. / Actually, it could have been a gun.
8. True This is a logical conclusion. Because she was envious of the family's money, it means that they had more money than she did.

7

must not to be → must not be
have got get → have got to get
can't getting → can't get
should have liked → should like
must had decided → must have decided
must have showed up → should have showed up

8

(Answers will vary.)

PART III NOUNS

UNIT 6 COUNT AND NON-COUNT NOUNS

1

study NC; breadth NC; thought NC; endeavor NC; languages C; dialects C; literatures C; thoughts C; language NC; time NC; language NC; space NC; communication NC

2

2. growth
3. business
4. information
5. friendliness
6. ease
7. transportation
8. availability
9. recreation
10. insurance
11. software
12. aerospace
13. technology
14. development
15. employment
16. investment
17. enterprise
18. science
19. medicine
20. oil
21. gas
22. travel
23. exploration
24. opportunity
25. expansion
26. brainpower

3

2. a bit of
3. a game of
4. a game of
5. a glass of
6. a slice of/a bit of
7. a serving of
8. a bit of/a slice of/a serving of
9. a slice of/a bit of/a serving of
10. a glass of
11. a bit of
12. a branch of
13. a clap of
14. a flash of
15. a bit of
16. a period of

4

2. a partner
3. integrity
4. work
5. great fun
6. love
7. practicality
8. a compatible companion
9. warmth
10. a career
11. a job
12. A good salary
13. respect

5

2. Production
3. ancient history
4. milk
5. A favorite dish
6. overcooked rice
7. snow
8. a symbol
9. wealth
10. ice
11. cream
12. a way
13. salt
14. the ices
15. music
16. a stick
17. happiness

6

history → the history
use → the use
smokes → smoke
communications → communication
a clay → clay
peoples → people
abstraction → abstractions
alphabet → alphabets
knowledges → knowledge

Answer Key

skill → skills
a literacy → literacy
informations → information
literacies → literacy

7

(Answers will vary.)

UNIT 7 DEFINITE AND INDEFINITE ARTICLES

1

2. a	9. an	16. a	23. 0
3. 0	10. a	17. a	24. an
4. the	11. 0	18. a	25. 0
5. 0	12. a	19. the	26. 0
6. 0	13. the	20. The	27. The
7. The	14. The	21. 0	
8. a	15. 0	22. the	

2

2. the	7. the	12. 0	17. 0
3. 0	8. 0	13. A	18. 0
4. 0	9. 0	14. a	
5. the	10. 0	15. a	
6. 0	11. 0	16. A	

3

2. a	10. a	18. a	26. 0
3. a	11. the	19. 0	27. 0
4. The	12. the	20. a	28. 0
5. the	13. the	21. The	29. the
6. the	14. The	22. the	30. 0
7. an	15. 0	23. a	31. 0
8. a	16. the	24. the	32. the
9. the	17. a	25. 0	

4

2. an	9. 0	16. the	23. 0
3. the	10. 0	17. a	24. 0
4. the	11. The	18. the	25. 0
5. an	12. 0	19. the	26. the
6. a	13. 0	20. the	27. the
7. The	14. The	21. a	28. 0
8. a	15. 0	22. 0	

5

2. the	7. the	12. 0	17. the
3. the	8. 0	13. the	18. the
4. the	9. 0	14. 0	19. the
5. 0	10. the	15. the	
6. the	11. 0	16. 0	

6

2. the	15. the	28. the	41. the
3. 0	16. The	29. the	42. the
4. 0	17. 0	30. the	43. a
5. the	18. 0	31. the	44. the
6. the	19. 0	32. the	45. 0
7. 0	20. the	33. the	46. a
8. 0	21. the	34. the	47. a
9. 0	22. the	35. the	48. the
10. the	23. the	36. The	49. a
11. 0	24. the	37. 0	50. 0
12. a	25. 0	38. a	
13. 0	26. the	39. the	
14. 0	27. the	40. the	

7

zoo → the zoo
the healthy → healthy
a satisfaction → the satisfaction
male → a male
A lion → The lion
the schoolchildren → schoolchildren
Arabian kind → the Arabian kind
Bactrian kind → the Bactrian kind
Chimpanzees → The chimpanzees
human family → a human family
the arguments → arguments
most popular animal → the most popular animal
zoo → the zoo
most expensive → the most expensive
the show → a show
a visitors → visitors
an applause → the applause
a life situation → the life situation
a zoo → the zoo
well-being → the well-being

8

(Answers may vary.)

UNIT 8 MODIFICATION OF NOUNS

1

2. some bright young
3. these new spring
4. many different international
5. the first exciting new
6. his long clean
7. much extra
8. expensive, fine silk/fine, expensive silk
9. some old Japanese
10. these simple, classic
11. elegant business

12. a soft, feminine
13. his wild, brightly colored
14. far-off, tropical South Sea
15. casual daytime
16. the liveliest new
17. Those hot pink
18. several brilliant purple
19. long, flowing cotton
20. any well-known contemporary
21. these fabulous new

2

2. flower gardens
3. vegetable gardens
4. work horses
5. show horses
6. house cats
7. family dogs
8. dog house
9. strawberry jam
10. blackberry tea
11. peach pie
12. kitchen table
13. childhood memories
14. childhood dreams
15. baby sister
16. summer night

3

2. one two-hundred-year-old dining room table
3. eight velvet-covered dining room chairs
4. two century-old Tiffany lamps
5. one silver-plated samovar
6. one leaded crystal chandelier
7. two (one) hundred-(and)-fifty-year-old rocking chairs
8. one hand-woven Persian carpet
9. one hand-written manuscript
10. three ivory-inlaid coffee tables
11. four hand-painted serving dishes
12. two hand-carved mahogany beds
13. two (one) hundred-(and)-thirty-year-old, gold-inlaid vases

4

2. local convenience store
3. students ethics council
4. international student activities
5. old, dilapidated houses
6. attention deficit disorder
7. Four-Year Service Award
8. Five-State Volunteerism Award

5

publising glamorous world → glamorous publishing world
southwest beautiful Montana → beautiful southwest Montana
blue, clear skies → clear, blue skies
gray, dirty smog → dirty, gray smog
respiratory mysterious ailment → mysterious respiratory ailment
ten-days siege → ten-day siege
four-rooms apartment → four-room apartment
dreary, jail, cement cell → dreary, cement jail cell
new prized job → prized new job
forty-two-years-old, feverish body → feverish, forty-two-year-old body (two mistakes)
Iron gigantic hammers → Gigantic iron hammers
black lead, huge weights → huge, black lead weights
two-hours rest → two-hour rest
New York unspeakably rude reception → unspeakably rude New York reception
three first weeks → first three weeks

6

(Answers will vary.)

UNIT 9 QUANTIFIERS

1

every
Certain
some
less
fewer
little
enough
all
No
either
more
a few
most of
much
plenty of
The amount of
a great deal of
neither of
A number of
none of
both
each of
more
many of

2

2. a few
3. a great deal of
4. a little
5. many
6. any
7. a bit of
8. all
9. A couple of
10. every
11. a bunch of
12. a couple of
13. most of
14. a lot of
15. a great deal of
16. a few of
17. a little

3

2. less
3. Many
4. a great deal of
5. Many
6. some
7. many
8. few
9. a lot of
10. some
11. a great number of

4

2. paycheck
3. time
4. expertise
5. professional advice
6. retirement
7. vacation
8. year
9. goals
10. professionals
11. specialty
12. insurance
13. expert
14. stock market
15. interests
16. money
17. trust

5

2. some
3. number
4. certain
5. many
6. Some
7. Some
8. Most of
9. an amount of
10. Either
11. a certain
12. less

6

Some of the errors may also be corrected in other ways.

A few people → Few people
either their immediate needs and their future needs → both their immediate needs and their future needs
fewer anxiety → less anxiety
many more money → much more money
every of your assets → all of your assets
the number of information → the amount of information
several advice → some advice
each of the news → all of the news
a few extra money → a little extra money
neither of those → either of those
a great deal of possible scenarios → a great number of possible scenarios
a great number of thought → a great deal of thought

7

(Answers will vary.)

PART IV ADJECTIVE CLAUSES AND PHRASES

UNIT 10 ADJECTIVE CLAUSES: REVIEW AND EXPANSION

1

whose creativity and persistence resulted in a very useful product
that covers up the mistakes you make when writing or typing
who began using tempera paint to cover up the typing errors in her work
that the type marks she typed onto the paper didn't erase as cleanly as those from manual typewriters
who was also an artist
which she called Mistake Out
she had bought for the backyard
which turned her down
which came to be called Liquid Paper
which ended about six months before she sold the company
of which $3.5 million was net income
she finally sold her business to Gillette in 1979
of whom she is understandably proud
which appeared on an NBC television show for several years in the mid-1960s
where he also directs some charities
whose purpose is to provide leading intellectuals with the time, space, and compatible colleagues
that they need to ponder and articulate the most important social problems of our era
that there was clearly a need for
which is a fine thing to do
everyone can appreciate
that will spread like wildfire
that Mrs. Graham gave to her product

2

2. whom
3. who
4. whom
5. where
6. which
7. who
8. 0
9. which
10. that
11. when
12. which
13. that
14. that
15. whose

3

2. which
3. who
4. whose
5. which
6. who
7. whose
8. who
9. who
10. who
11. when
12. who
13. who
14. whose
15. who
16. that
17. whom

4

2. which
3. where
4. who/that
5. which/that
6. whom/that/0
7. which/that/0
8. that/which/0
9. whose
10. who/that
11. when
12. which/that
13. which/that
14. which/that
15. which/that/0

5

2. who/that feels energized around others
3. whose energies are activated by being alone
4. who/that pay attention to details in the world
5. who/that is more interested in relationships between people and things
6. that/which/0 this test measures
7. who/that made decisions objectively
8. whose primary way to reach a conclusion
9. who/that took other people's feelings into consideration
10. that/which/0 he or she has
11. which we prefer to live or work
12. who/that prefer a planned and predictable environment
13. that/which/0 they find themselves in *or* in which they find themselves
14. whose life must be planned in advance
15. where he should be placed *or* in which he should be placed *or* that/which/0 he should be placed in to most enhance the company
16. which you would be the happiest and most productive

6

2. B
3. A
4. B
5. A
6. B
7. A
8. B
9. A
10. A
11. B
12. B

7

some of them → some of which
whom is nervous → who is nervous
whom rarely smiles → who rarely smiles
to which everything is serious → to whom everything is serious
who they are → who are
whom often suffered → who often suffered
of that others → of whom others
which is probably not → who is probably not
they were born under it → they were born under
who born → who was born
that born → that was born
that are intuitive → who are intuitive
who they are → who are

whose their abilities → whose abilities
to improve it → to improve
for people are looking → for people who are looking
which it is → which is

8

(Answers will vary.)

UNIT 11 ADJECTIVE CLAUSES WITH QUANTIFIERS; ADJECTIVAL MODIFYING PHRASES

1

Adjective Clauses: many of which were filmed in remote parts of the world; one of which was called *A Trip to the Moon* and influenced many subsequent filmmakers; some of which involved chase scenes

Adjective Phrases: learning how to fake prizefights, news events, and foreign settings; made with the aid of the microscope; credited with creating methods; leading toward the development of special-effects movies; shot outdoors; a camera operator and director; showing different actions simultaneously; seen and loved even today; changing the world forever

2

2. most of which could have been avoided
3. half of which are longer than 40 days
4. 71 percent of whom think people in power take advantage of others
5. 14 percent of whom achieve scores of over 130 on IQ tests
6. more than half of whom are under 64 years of age
7. all of which yield more nutrients when lightly cooked than when raw
8. much of which is junk food

3

2. transformed by a magic spell
3. taking on a big insurance company
4. investigating
5. starring Leonardo DiCaprio and Kate Winslet
6. centering on a love affair
7. adapted from the TV series
8. full of cash
9. sure to delight every member of the family
10. enlisted to impersonate the president of the United States

4

(suggested answers)

2. Instead of traditional seating, cinema pubs contain independent sections of tables and comfortable swivel chairs, allowing you to feel like you are in your own living room.
3. One of the servers, most of whom are local college students, comes to each table before the movie begins and takes your order for food and beverages.
4. The ambience in the theater is similar to that in a cabaret, where there is an intimate feeling.
5. In accordance with the cozy atmosphere, the cinema pubs show small films, many of which are foreign.
6. Although you have come to the theater to see a movie, you will also find that the cinema pub is a good place where people like to socialize.
7. In fact, there are cinema pubs, known as places where discriminating singles can go to meet each other, in certain areas.
8. The idea of the cinema pub, already popular in the United Kingdom, is beginning to catch on in the United States.
9. Cinema pubs show recent films in a relaxed atmosphere, making them a welcome alternative to huge and impersonal movie multiplexes.
10. For a change of pace, look in the newspaper for a cinema pub in your city.

5

some of them → some of which
making in 1945 → made in 1945
that produced for entertainment value → produced for entertainment value
showed the harshness of life → showing the harshness of life
was an outstanding director → an outstanding director
the most famous of them is → the most famous of which is
which a movie → a movie
calling the "New Wave" → called the "New Wave"
seeing in movies → seen in movies
was known as the "Angry Young Man" movement → known as the "Angry Young Man" movement
some of them are masterfully explored → some of which are masterfully explored
was the first Asian filmmaker → the first Asian filmmaker
portray the problems of the individual → portraying the problems of the individual
included Shakespeare's plays → including Shakespeare's plays

6

(Answers will vary.)

PART V PASSIVE VOICE

UNIT 12 THE PASSIVE: REVIEW AND EXPANSION

1

Storyville School: were stolen; were left; was still being sought; could not be contacted
Restaurant Burglarized: was burglarized; had been altered; have been broken into; is being made; will be arrested; going to have . . . installed
Barking Dog: was filed; is always being disturbed; should not be forced; to have . . . removed; cannot be reached; is being cared for
Cash Register: was fired; arrested; to have . . . documented; to have . . . barred; is estimated

2

2. will be caressed
3. laze
4. savor
5. will be thrilled
6. must be seen
7. must be enjoyed
8. are spoken
9. will be delighted
10. was settled
11. were enchanted
12. left
13. can experience
14. speak
15. will be enchanted
16. was colonized
17. are not allowed
18. may be rented
19. are imported/have been imported

3

2. would actually be employed
3. is sustained
4. were sent
5. are maintained
6. must be controlled
7. cannot be grown
8. is obscured
9. has to be done
10. has been produced
11. is recycled

Answer Key

12. gets used
13. have been utilized
14. maximized
15. were developed
16. am known
17. are made
18. is found
19. have it collected
20. is filtered
21. is being built
22. will be completed

4

Identifications:
2. had ever had the heads of the tape player cleaned
3. had some furniture sent
4. have it shortened; have future alterations done
5. have had it checked
6. had had a car sent

New Causatives:
2. should have the tapes transferred to regular cassettes
3. have your table looked at by an insurance adjuster
4. have the bill sent to him
5. will have the problem fixed
6. have your son picked up

5

2. get my car fixed
3. got towed
4. got charged
5. got stolen
6. got dumped
7. get hired
8. gets asked
9. get fired

6

1b. They can be toasted easily.
 c. They were introduced to Mexico by the Spanish.
 d. And before that, they had been brought to Spain by the Moors.
2a. Pepitas are ground for use in sauces.
 b. They also are eaten whole.
 c. Even if they have been ground, the sauce has a rough texture.
 d. Pepitas have been used since pre-Columbian times.
3a. In Mexico, it is made of unsmoked meat and spices.
 b. In Spain, the meat is smoked.
4a. Street vendors in Mexico sell jicama in thick slices that have been sprinkled with salt, lime juice, and chili powder.
5a. Avocados are considered a true delicacy.
 b. If they are hard, they should be allowed to ripen.
 c. Guacamole is made from avocados.
 d. Avocados also are used in salads and as a garnish.
6a. Meat is steamed in little packets of banana leaves.
 b. First, they must be softened over a flame.
 c. Then, the meat and other ingredients are wrapped in them.
7a. They are cooked in various ways, including deep-frying and baking.
 b. Firm green bananas may be substituted.
8a. They can be eaten with any meal.
 b. They are made from corn or wheat flour.
 c. Frozen tortillas can now be found in supermarkets.
9a. Chilies are used to season many different dishes.
 b. Chili-seasoned foods have been consumed for more than 8,000 years.
10a. Corn is used widely in Mexico.
 b. In Mexican cooking, no part of the corn is wasted.
 c. The ears, husks, silk, and kernels are used in different ways.
 d. This was the first plant that was cultivated in Mexico.

7

which also known → which is also known
have been occurred → have occurred
has never found → has never been found
have been proposing → have been proposed
have proven → have been proven
have frequently been record → have frequently been recorded
has been find → has been found
usually are form → usually are formed
draw by → are drawn by

8

(Answers will vary.)

UNIT 13 REPORTING IDEAS AND FACTS WITH PASSIVES

1

are believed
is now known
is now understood
are regarded
are assumed
has been found
had been considered
was reported
is recommended
are known
are suggested
are considered

2

2. is believed
3. was previously thought
4. is understood
5. is well known
6. would be perceived
7. is widely confirmed
8. has been well established
9. are known
10. has been considered
11. can be asssumed

3

2. is believed
3. is claimed
4. are reported
5. is not known
6. is now assumed
7. is also thought
8. was conjectured
9. are now believed
10. is said
11. is known
12. is known
13. is now thought
14. can safely be assumed

4

believes to go further → is believed to go further
been recognized → have been recognized

is no longer consider → is no longer considered
are now considering → are now considered
has eliminated → has been eliminated
now prohibited → is now prohibited
have made → have been made
is still thinking → is still thought
hasn't been doing → hasn't been done
is considering → is considered
has now been establishing → has now been established
it also know → it is also known
feels → is felt
is assumes → is assumed
are regard → are regarded
fined → are fined
jailed → are jailed
will need → will be needed
not permitted → is not permitted
have established → have been established
are being educating → are being educated
is conjecturing → is conjectured
will been almost eliminated → will have been almost eliminated

5

(Answers will vary.

TEST: UNITS 1-3

PART ONE

DIRECTIONS: Circle the letter of the correct answer to complete each sentence.

EXAMPLE:

Dolphins, _____ porpoises, are well known for their ability to delight humans with their antics.   A B (C) D
- (A) alike
- (B) that they are like
- (C) like
- (D) which are alike

1. Construction of the Brooklyn Bridge, the first steel-wire suspension bridge in the world, _____ in 1869 but wasn't finished until 1893.   A B C D
   - (A) was beginning
   - (B) has begun
   - (C) began
   - (D) beginning

2. By the time the monorail is completed next year, the taxpayers _____ over twenty-two million dollars for a transportation system that is already obsolete.   A B C D
   - (A) will spend
   - (B) will be spending
   - (C) will have spent
   - (D) will have been spending

3. Since the use of antibiotics _____ widespread, certain types of pneumonia and streptococcal infections are no longer as terrifying as they once were.   A B C D
   - (A) was becoming
   - (B) has become
   - (C) had become
   - (D) becomes

4. By the time the ancient Egyptian civilization began to flourish more than 5,000 years ago, the onion _____ a staple food throughout the Middle East for many years.   A B C D
   - (A) had already been
   - (B) was already
   - (C) has already been
   - (D) would have been

Test: Units 1–3

5. Because the river _____ steadily since Sunday, the residents of the area have been advised to prepare for flood conditions.
   (A) rose
   (B) had risen
   (C) is rising
   (D) has been rising

   A B C D

6. The best diamonds are transparent and colorless, but they actually _____ in color from clear to black.
   (A) range
   (B) are ranging
   (C) ranged
   (D) have been ranging

   A B C D

7. Astonishingly, in 1998 the citizens of Minnesota elected a governor who _____ a professional wrestler.
   (A) would be
   (B) used to be
   (C) have been
   (D) Both A and B

   A B C D

8. Although popular computer use exploded throughout the world in the 1990s, academics _____ by computer since the early 1970s.
   (A) communicated
   (B) had been communicating
   (C) are communicating
   (D) used to communicate

   A B C D

9. Small children who witnessed Halley's Comet in 1986 might see it again when it _____ in the skies in 2061.
   (A) is appearing
   (B) will appear
   (C) will be appearing
   (D) appears

   A B C D

10. By analyzing historical and current data, meteorologists can predict the number of hurricanes that _____ in the Caribbean in any given year.
    (A) will appear
    (B) are going to appear
    (C) are appearing
    (D) Both A and B

    A B C D

Part Two

DIRECTIONS: Each sentence has four underlined words or phrases. The four underlined parts of the sentence are marked A, B, C, and D. Circle the letter of the <u>one</u> underlined word or phrase that is NOT CORRECT.

Example:

People in <u>every part</u> of the world now <u>readily</u> and easily
            A   B
<u>communicates</u> <u>by means</u> of electronic mail.
    C   D

A B (C) D

11. Because the beaches <u>are eroding</u> at an alarming rate for the <u>past</u> ten
                                    A   B
years, the state government <u>no longer</u> <u>permits</u> building within 100
                                    C   D
yards of the coastal area.

A B C D

12. The Rosetta Stone, which <u>is</u> a large piece of stone that priests
                                                         A
<u>have inscribed</u> more than 2,000 years ago, <u>was</u> discovered by
   B   C

Napoleon's troops in 1799 and <u>has provided</u> scholars with the key
                                           D

to deciphering Egyptian hieroglyphics.

13. The Mayan Indians, archaeologists <u>are thinking</u>, <u>originated</u> around
                                    A   B

1000 B.C. in northern Guatemala, where evidence of an early

agricultural people <u>has been</u> <u>found</u>.
                       C   D

14. Before the construction of the English Chunnel, which <u>connects</u>
                                                  A

France and England, most people <u>didn't</u> <u>believe</u> that travel by land
                                B   C

between the two countries <u>will</u> be possible in the twentieth century.
                             D

15. When banks <u>failed</u> and stocks <u>fell</u> precipitously on Black Monday in
              A   B

1929, many Wall Street investors <u>were jumping</u> from their office
                                       C

windows to their deaths, reacting in panic to what they <u>perceived</u>
                                                    D

as financial ruin.

16. When the earthquake <u>occurred</u> at 3:49 A.M., most people in the city
                            A

<u>slept</u> in their beds at home and so <u>escaped</u> the injuries that a few
 B   C

<u>suffered</u> from collapsing bridges and crumbling highways.
  D

17. These days, doctors <u>are seeing</u> more children who <u>suffer</u> from asthma,
                          A   B

which <u>was used to be</u> quite rare among children who <u>were</u> otherwise
      C   D

healthy.

18. During the past decade, retail sales from mail order companies that

also <u>have</u> a presence on the Internet <u>were quadrupling</u> as people <u>take</u>
    A   B   C

advantage of the convenience of <u>shopping</u> from home.
                                     D

Test: Units 1–3

19. <u>By</u> the time the sailors in the famous Whitbread competition <u>reach</u>   **A B C D**
      A   B

   their final destination, they <u>will be traveling</u> over ocean waters <u>for</u>
                                               C   D

   more than six months.

20. The term "baby boomers" <u>refers</u> to the exploding population of   **A B C D**
                                         A

   babies that <u>had been</u> <u>born</u> in the years just after World War II <u>ended</u>.
                 B   C   D

Test: Units 4-5

Part One

DIRECTIONS: *Circle the letter of the correct answer to complete each sentence.*

Example:

Dolphins, _____ porpoises, are well known for their ability to delight humans with their antics.   A B (C) D
- (A) alike
- (B) that they are like
- (C) like
- (D) which are alike

1. Although many spectators believed that the Australian gymnast, with her amazing flexibility and control, _____ the gold medal, the Olympic judges awarded it to the Romanian instead.   A B C D
   - (A) must have won
   - (B) should have won
   - (C) had to win
   - (D) won

2. Before the construction of the Panama Canal, ships _____ around the tip of South America to get to the Pacific Ocean from the Atlantic Ocean.   A B C D
   - (A) should have traveled
   - (B) must have traveled
   - (C) had to travel
   - (D) have traveled

3. It seems obvious, when looking at a map, that the eastern part of Brazil _____ connected to Africa long ago when the earth was forming.   A B C D
   - (A) must be
   - (B) must have been
   - (C) should have been
   - (D) might be

4. The mayor told the townspeople that _____ drink the water until the laboratory declared it safe again.   A B C D
   - (A) they didn't have to
   - (B) they'd rather not
   - (C) they'd better not
   - (D) they weren't supposed to

T5

5. It is generally agreed that when you travel in countries other than your own, you _____ conform to the local customs as much as possible.
   (A) could
   (B) might
   (C) may
   (D) should

6. The financial advisor told her client that he _____ invest in a money market fund or he _____ invest in municipal bonds—either way would be safe.
   (A) could / could
   (B) must / must
   (C) could / must
   (D) must / could

7. Residents of the apartment complex _____ rent a reserved parking space at $45 per month if they wish.
   (A) must
   (B) may
   (C) might
   (D) have got to

8. Anorexia nervosa is a disease afflicting young women who believe that they _____ be as thin as the models in the fashion magazines.
   (A) had better
   (B) have got to
   (C) could
   (D) ought

9. The botanists knew that the tree _____ be about 750 years old because it displayed the number of rings to indicate that.
   (A) had to
   (B) could
   (C) was supposed to
   (D) should

10. All the experts believe that the horse from Kentucky _____ win the big race next Saturday because of his breeding, his endurance, and his training.
    (A) is supposed to
    (B) has to
    (C) must
    (D) should

Part Two

DIRECTIONS: *Each sentence has four underlined words or phrases. The four underlined parts of the sentence are marked A, B, C, and D. Circle the letter of the <u>one</u> underlined word or phrase that is NOT CORRECT.*

Example:

People in <u>every part</u> of the world now <u>readily</u> and easily
          A   B
<u>communicates</u> <u>by means</u> of electronic mail.
     C   D

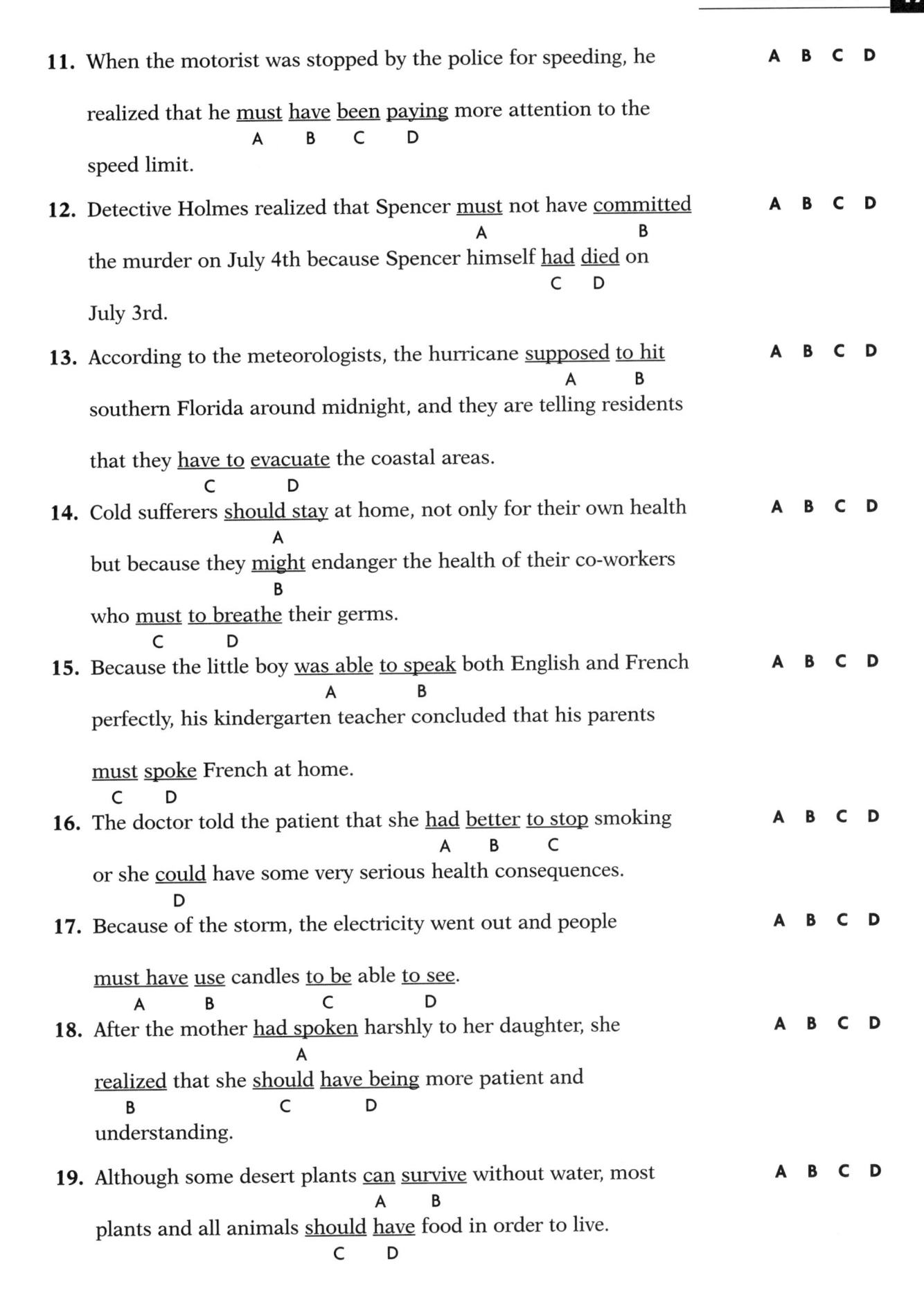

11. When the motorist was stopped by the police for speeding, he

realized that he <u>must</u> <u>have</u> <u>been</u> <u>paying</u> more attention to the
                     A   B   C   D

speed limit.   A B C D

12. Detective Holmes realized that Spencer <u>must</u> not have <u>committed</u>
                                          A   B

the murder on July 4th because Spencer himself <u>had</u> <u>died</u> on
                                                     C   D

July 3rd.

13. According to the meteorologists, the hurricane <u>supposed</u> <u>to hit</u>
                                                           A   B

southern Florida around midnight, and they are telling residents

that they <u>have to</u> <u>evacuate</u> the coastal areas.
            C   D

14. Cold sufferers <u>should stay</u> at home, not only for their own health
                           A

but because they <u>might</u> endanger the health of their co-workers
                     B

who <u>must</u> <u>to breathe</u> their germs.
     C   D

15. Because the little boy <u>was able</u> <u>to speak</u> both English and French
                       A   B

perfectly, his kindergarten teacher concluded that his parents

<u>must</u> <u>spoke</u> French at home.
 C   D

16. The doctor told the patient that she <u>had</u> <u>better</u> <u>to stop</u> smoking
                                   A   B   C

or she <u>could</u> have some very serious health consequences.
       D

17. Because of the storm, the electricity went out and people

<u>must have</u> <u>use</u> candles <u>to be</u> able <u>to see</u>.
   A   B   C   D

18. After the mother <u>had spoken</u> harshly to her daughter, she
                     A

<u>realized</u> that she <u>should</u> <u>have being</u> more patient and
   B   C   D

understanding.

19. Although some desert plants <u>can</u> <u>survive</u> without water, most
                              A   B

plants and all animals <u>should</u> <u>have</u> food in order to live.
                     C   D

20. Nobody knows what happened to the Mayan civilization about A.D.   A B C D

800, but some researchers <u>believe</u> that fierce, warlike enemies

                                              A

<u>might</u> <u>had</u> <u>driven</u> them from their homes.
  B   C   D

TEST: UNITS 6–9

PART ONE

DIRECTIONS: *Circle the letter of the correct answer to complete each sentence.*

EXAMPLE:

Dolphins, _____ porpoises, are well known for their ability to delight humans with their antics.   A B (C) D
(A) alike
(B) that they are like
(C) like
(D) which are alike

1. Because of the emphasis on nutrition in recent decades, Americans now consume _____ chicken and fish and much less beef.   A B C D
   (A) a number of
   (B) a great deal of
   (C) either
   (D) many

2. On much of television today, _____ more frequently presented than straightforward information.   A B C D
   (A) a sensational news is
   (B) sensational news is
   (C) sensational news are
   (D) some sensational news are

3. There are few, if any, _____ more important than honesty in the assessment of a person's character.   A B C D
   (A) criterion that is
   (B) criteria that are
   (C) criterias that is
   (D) criterions that are

4. _____ certain molds and fungi to multiply very rapidly.   A B C D
   (A) A tropical weather causes
   (B) Tropical weather cause
   (C) The tropical weather cause
   (D) Tropical weather causes

5. After the flood, many schools remained closed for several days because of the concern about _____ .   A B C D
   (A) a health
   (B) some health
   (C) children health
   (D) health

6. A false stereotype that used to exist was that _____ usually tense and nervous.
   (A) thin people is
   (B) a thin people is
   (C) thin people are
   (D) thin peoples are

7. Augusta Ada Byron, _____, created a program for a theoretical computer in the mid-nineteenth century.
   (A) an English visionary woman mathematician
   (B) a visionary English woman mathematician
   (C) an English woman visionary mathematician
   (D) a visionary English mathematician woman

8. The Great Depression of 1929 caused the loss of millions of _____ almost impossible to find.
   (A) the jobs, and the work was
   (B) job, and work was
   (C) jobs, and work was
   (D) jobs, and works were

9. Although a third party has exhibited some political strength from time to time, the United States essentially has _____ political system.
   (A) two parties
   (B) a two parties
   (C) the two parties'
   (D) a two-party

10. Not _____ from South Africa, although most of the world's supply does originate there.
    (A) every gold comes
    (B) all gold come
    (C) all gold comes
    (D) every gold come

PART TWO

DIRECTIONS: *Each sentence has four underlined words or phrases. The four underlined parts of the sentence are marked A, B, C, and D. Circle the letter of the <u>one</u> underlined word or phrase that is NOT CORRECT.*

EXAMPLE:

People in <u>every part</u> of the world now <u>readily</u> and easily
            A   B
<u>communicates</u> <u>by means</u> of electronic mail.
      C   D

A B (C) D

11. <u>Horses</u> races are recorded as early as 1500 B.C. in Egypt, but
    A
the organized <u>sport</u> <u>dates</u> from <u>twelfth-century</u> England.
                B   C   D

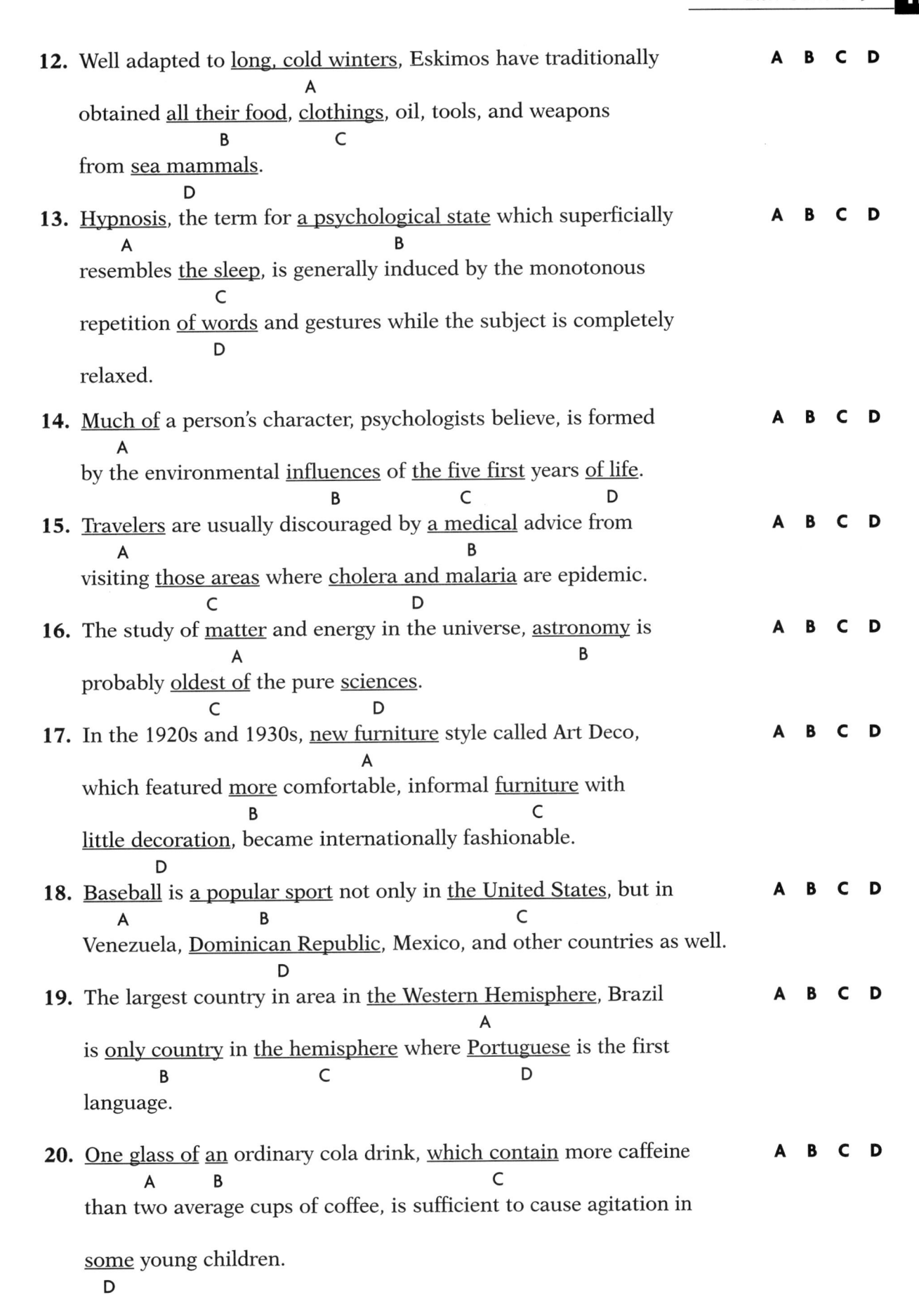

Test: Units 6–9

12. Well adapted to <u>long, cold winters</u>, Eskimos have traditionally
                    A
    obtained <u>all their food</u>, <u>clothings</u>, oil, tools, and weapons
            B   C
    from <u>sea mammals</u>.
            D

    A B C D

13. <u>Hypnosis</u>, the term for <u>a psychological state</u> which superficially
       A   B
    resembles <u>the sleep</u>, is generally induced by the monotonous
             C
    repetition <u>of words</u> and gestures while the subject is completely
            D
    relaxed.

    A B C D

14. <u>Much of</u> a person's character, psychologists believe, is formed
      A
    by the environmental <u>influences</u> of <u>the five first</u> years <u>of life</u>.
                      B   C   D

    A B C D

15. <u>Travelers</u> are usually discouraged by <u>a medical</u> advice from
      A   B
    visiting <u>those areas</u> where <u>cholera and malaria</u> are epidemic.
          C   D

    A B C D

16. The study of <u>matter</u> and energy in the universe, <u>astronomy</u> is
          A   B
    probably <u>oldest of</u> the pure <u>sciences</u>.
        C   D

    A B C D

17. In the 1920s and 1930s, <u>new furniture</u> style called Art Deco,
                              A
    which featured <u>more</u> comfortable, informal <u>furniture</u> with
                   B   C
    <u>little decoration</u>, became internationally fashionable.
        D

    A B C D

18. <u>Baseball</u> is <u>a popular sport</u> not only in <u>the United States</u>, but in
     A   B   C
    Venezuela, <u>Dominican Republic</u>, Mexico, and other countries as well.
                   D

    A B C D

19. The largest country in area in <u>the Western Hemisphere</u>, Brazil
                                    A
    is <u>only country</u> in <u>the hemisphere</u> where <u>Portuguese</u> is the first
       B   C   D
    language.

    A B C D

20. <u>One glass of</u> <u>an</u> ordinary cola drink, <u>which contain</u> more caffeine
        A   B   C
    than two average cups of coffee, is sufficient to cause agitation in
    <u>some</u> young children.
     D

    A B C D

TEST: UNITS 10–11

PART ONE

DIRECTIONS: Circle the letter of the correct answer to complete each sentence.

EXAMPLE:

Dolphins, _____ porpoises, are well known for their ability to delight humans with their antics.   A B (C) D
(A) alike
(B) that they are like
(C) like
(D) which are alike

1. Tulips, _____ into Holland in 1554, were quickly and highly valued, and by the 1630s they became the objects of wild financial speculation in Europe.   A B C D
   (A) which introduced
   (B) that they were introduced
   (C) which introduced them
   (D) introduced

2. Concepts of modern nursing were founded by Florence Nightingale, an English nurse _____ to the care of the sick and the war-wounded.   A B C D
   (A) that she dedicated her life
   (B) whose life she dedicated
   (C) whose life was dedicated
   (D) whose life she dedicated it

3. Relics _____ accidentally while constructing a new subway line in Mexico City yielded new information about previous civilizations in the area.   A B C D
   (A) that workers found them
   (B) which workers they found
   (C) that they were found by workers
   (D) that workers found

4. The advanced course in astrophysics will be open only to those graduate students _____ a grade point average of 3.8 or above.   A B C D
   (A) having
   (B) they will have
   (C) have
   (D) whom have

T12

5. Cork, the second largest city in Ireland, is the site of many industries, _____ automobile manufacturing and whiskey distilling.
   (A) two of them are
   (B) which two are
   (C) two of which are
   (D) of which are two

6. Ships traveling in the North Atlantic during the winter must be constantly vigilant to avoid icebergs, large masses of ice _____ only one-ninth is visible above water.
   (A) which
   (B) of which
   (C) that
   (D) of that

7. The Olympic Games, _____ in 776 B.C., did not include women participants until 1912.
   (A) they were first played
   (B) first played
   (C) that they were first played
   (D) which they were first played

8. One of the great fiction writers in English, Charles Dickens portrays all aspects of societal abuses, _____ child labor, debt imprisonment, and legal injustices.
   (A) which are including
   (B) that they include
   (C) included
   (D) including

9. *The Mikado,* a warm-hearted spoof of a country _____, is one of the best-loved works of the English operetta composers Gilbert and Sullivan.
   (A) which they knew nothing about
   (B) that they knew nothing about it
   (C) about that they knew nothing
   (D) they know nothing about it

10. Few visitors to Disney World in Florida are aware that much of its electrical power comes from the energy _____ by burning its own garbage.
    (A) that produces
    (B) producing
    (C) which it is produced
    (D) it produces

PART TWO

DIRECTIONS: *Each sentence has four underlined words or phrases. The four underlined parts of the sentence are marked A, B, C, and D. Circle the letter of the* one *underlined word or phrase that is NOT CORRECT.*

EXAMPLE:

People in <u>every part</u> of the world now <u>readily</u> and easily
           A   B
<u>communicates</u> <u>by means</u> of electronic mail.
    C   D

Test: Units 10–11

11. South of San Francisco lies a region now <u>known as</u> Silicon Valley,   **A B C D**
                                                           A
<u>which</u> name alludes to the silicon <u>used</u> in the many high-technology
  B   C
industries <u>located</u> there.
               D

12. Sunlight sometimes filters through rain droplets in a certain way   **A B C D**

    <u>that combines</u> to form a rainbow, which <u>it is</u> an arc <u>composed</u> of
         A   B   C
    every color in the spectrum, and is <u>regarded</u> in many places of the
                                             D
    world as an omen of good luck.

13. Japanese, <u>which spoken</u> by more than 100 million people,   **A B C D**
               A
    <u>most of whom live</u> in Japan, appears to be unrelated to <u>any other</u>
            B   C
    language <u>spoken</u> in Asia.
            D

14. Genius is a term <u>which</u> may be used to describe a person <u>who</u>   **A B C D**
                    A   B
    <u>he has</u> a high intelligence or a special aptitude <u>in a certain field</u>.
      C   D

15. In a medical study of nearly 5,000 adults, <u>half of them</u> were given   **A B C D**
                                                            A
    one aspirin a day and the other half <u>given</u> a placebo, it was found
                                            B
    that those <u>taking</u> aspirin suffered 38 percent fewer heart attacks
                  C
    than those <u>who weren't</u>.
                D

16. A fact <u>not widely known</u> is <u>that</u> Theodore Roosevelt, <u>that was</u> a   **A B C D**
            A   B   C
    robust and boisterous outdoorsman, had been a weak and sickly

    child <u>who suffered</u> from asthma.
         D

17. In recent decades, educated women have been marrying later,   **A B C D**

    <u>that</u> means <u>that they</u> have fewer years <u>in</u> <u>which</u> to produce offspring.
     A   B   C   D

18. The Industrial Revolution is a term <u>which</u> <u>is</u> usually applied to the   **A B C D**
                                          A B
    social and economic changes <u>that</u> <u>they mark</u> the transition of
                                    C   D
    society from an agricultural one to an industrial one.

19. Spaghetti, widely <u>believed</u> to be a dish <u>originating</u> in Italy, was   A B C D
                                  A   B

actually brought there by Marco Polo from China, <u>to where</u> he
                                                                C

had <u>traveled</u> at the end of the thirteenth century.
           D

20. Many older couples, at a time <u>when they</u> are still healthy and   A B C D
                                               A

active, move to a retirement community in order to meet people

<u>with whom</u> to socialize, and to participate in activities <u>they</u> <u>enjoy them</u>.
     B   C   D

Test: Units 12–13

Part One

DIRECTIONS: *Circle the letter of the correct answer to complete each sentence.*

Example:

Dolphins, _____ porpoises, are well known for their ability to delight humans with their antics.   A B (C) D

(A) alike
(B) that they are like
(C) like
(D) which are alike

1. In the cultivation of bonzai trees, the plants _____ small and in true proportion to their natural models by growing them in small containers.   A B C D

   (A) keep
   (B) are keeping
   (C) are kept
   (D) kept

2. When tornadoes _____ over water, they are called waterspouts.   A B C D

   (A) are occurring
   (B) occur
   (C) are occurred
   (D) have occurred

3. The Great Wall of China was the only man-made structure on earth which _____ when they were circling the earth.   A B C D

   (A) could see by the astronauts
   (B) could be seen by the astronauts
   (C) the astronauts could be seen
   (D) could see the astronauts

4. In spite of the severity of the crash, no one _____, which is attributed to the fact that all four passengers were wearing their seat belts.   A B C D

   (A) was even slightly injuring
   (B) that they were slightly injured
   (C) even slightly injured
   (D) was even slightly injured

5. The characters of the novelist Isaac Bashevis Singer suffer frequently from loneliness and alienation and _____.
   (A) tormented by demons
   (B) are tormenting by demons
   (C) are tormented by demons
   (D) been tormented by demons

   A B C D

6. By the mid-twenty-first century the last veterans of the war _____, finally putting to rest the bitterness that followed it.
   (A) will have been died
   (B) will be died
   (C) will have died
   (D) will died

   A B C D

7. In a most spectacular manifestation of computer crime, the defendant _____ to have stolen $47 million from banks and securities firms.
   (A) is alleged
   (B) alleges
   (C) has alleged
   (D) being alleged

   A B C D

8. Cloisonné, a method of decorating metal surfaces with enamel, _____ in the Middle East and perfected by the Chinese, Japanese, and French.
   (A) probably invented
   (B) was probably invented
   (C) had probably invented
   (D) must have invented

   A B C D

9. Until after World War II, when many foreign-made cars began to be popular, almost all the automobiles driven in the United States _____.
   (A) made in Detroit by automobile workers
   (B) had been made in Detroit
   (C) were made in Detroit by automobile workers
   (D) made in Detroit

   A B C D

10. Rasputin _____ responsible for many of the ill-fated events that occurred during the reign of Czar Nicholas II in Russia.
    (A) believed to be
    (B) was believed to have been
    (C) they believed him to be
    (D) was believing to be

    A B C D

PART TWO

DIRECTIONS: Each sentence has four underlined words or phrases. The four underlined parts of the sentence are marked A, B, C, and D. Circle the letter of the <u>one</u> underlined word or phrase that is NOT CORRECT.

EXAMPLE:

People in <u>every part</u> of the world now <u>readily</u> and easily
              A   B
<u>communicates</u> <u>by means</u> of electronic mail.
       C   D

A B (C) D

T18 Test: Units 12–13

11. In northern <u>climates</u>, <u>it considered</u> of prime importance to get the   **A B C D**
             A   B
    <u>crops harvested</u> by mid-October, before the heavy winter
         C
    <u>snowstorms arrive</u>.
         D

12. The modern horse <u>evolved</u> in North America, <u>spread</u> all over the   **A B C D**
                A   B
    world, and <u>hunted</u> by early man and <u>domesticated</u> by Asian nomads
          C   D
    as early as the third millennium B.C.

13. Outsourcing is a phenomenon of the late twentieth century <u>in which</u>   **A B C D**
                                                A
    certain tasks <u>are no longer performing</u> by company employees, but
                B
    <u>by independent contractors</u> who <u>are compensated</u> at a lower rate.
         C   D

14. <u>Resembling</u> the giraffe to which <u>it is related</u>, the okapi <u>is find</u> in the   **A B C D**
        A   B   C
    rain forests of the upper Congo River and <u>was unknown</u> to zoologists
                                              D
    until the early twentieth century.

15. In Shakespeare's famous drama, which <u>is known</u> to be <u>based</u> on fact,   **A B C D**
                                          A   B
    Macbeth seizes the Scottish throne by killing Duncan in battle

    and <u>is then defeated</u> and <u>kill</u> by Duncan's son.
         C   D

16. It <u>has long been suspected</u> that <u>consuming</u> large quantities of fish   **A B C D**
          A   B
    <u>raises</u> the level of intelligence, but this theory has <u>never proved</u>.
     C   D

17. It could never <u>have predicted</u> that the group of four <u>young British</u>   **A B C D**
                  A   B
    rock musicians <u>would attain</u> such popularity after they <u>had been seen</u>
               C   D
    only once on American television.

18. Before photography <u>was invented</u>, people of means <u>had</u> their   **A B C D**
                       A   B
    pictures <u>painting</u> by famous artists so that their images
         C
    <u>would be remembered</u> forever.
         D

19. Japanese artists have long <u>being</u> <u>inspired</u> by Mount Fuji, the   **A B C D**
                                        A   B

mountain which is <u>considered</u> sacred in Japan and is a volcano
                             C

with a perfectly <u>formed</u> snow-capped cone.
                       D

20. The police <u>are still mystified</u> by the lack of clues regarding the   **A B C D**
                          A

kidnapping, which <u>must have committed</u> <u>by a person</u> who
                                B   C

<u>was known</u> to the victims.
     D

Answer Key for Tests

NOTE: *Correct responses for Part Two questions appear in parentheses.*

Answer Key for Test: UNITS 1–3

Part One
1. C
2. C
3. B
4. A
5. D
6. A
7. B
8. B
9. D
10. D

Part Two
11. A (have been eroding)
12. B (inscribed)
13. A (think)
14. D (would)
15. C (jumped)
16. B (were sleeping)
17. C (used to be)
18. C (took)
19. C (will have traveled/will have been traveling)
20. B (were)

Answer Key for Test: UNITS 4–5

Part One
1. B
2. C
3. B
4. C
5. D
6. A
7. B
8. B
9. A
10. D

Part Two
11. A (should)
12. A (could)
13. A (was supposed)
14. D (breathe)
15. D (speak)
16. C (stop)
17. A (had to)
18. D (have been)
19. C (must)
20. C (have)

Answer Key for Test: UNITS 6–9

Part One
1. B
2. B
3. B
4. D
5. D
6. C
7. B
8. C
9. D
10. C

Part Two
11. A (Horse)
12. C (clothing)
13. C (sleep)
14. C (the first five)
15. B (medical)
16. C (the oldest of)
17. A (a new furniture)
18. D (the Dominican Republic)
19. B (the only country)
20. C (which contains)

Answer Key for Test: UNITS 10–11

Part One
1. D
2. C
3. D
4. A
5. C
6. B
7. B
8. D
9. A
10. D

Part Two
11. B (whose)
12. B (is)
13. A (which is spoken)
14. C (has)
15. A (half of whom)
16. C (who was)
17. A (which)
18. D (mark)
19. C (where)
20. D (enjoy)

Answer Key for Test: UNITS 12–13

Part One
1. C
2. B
3. B
4. D
5. C
6. C
7. A
8. B
9. B
10. B

Part Two
11. B (it is considered)
12. C (was hunted)
13. B (are no longer performed)
14. C (is found)
15. D (killed)
16. D (never been proved/proven)
17. A (have been predicted)
18. C (painted)
19. A (been)
20. B (must have been committed)